Remote Learning Strategies for Students with IEPs

This succinct guidebook provides educators with the essentials they need to navigate remote learning for students with Individualized Education Programs (IEPs). Filled with practical tools and excerpts from teachers in the field, this book explores tips to share with parents, alongside synchronous and asynchronous strategies that can help make IEPs possible in a remote environment. Ideal for special educators, coaches, service providers, and leaders, this is the go-to resource for supporting IEPs outside the traditional classroom.

Kathryn A. Welby is Director of Teacher Preparation and Assistant Professor of Practice at Merrimack College, USA. She holds Massachusetts licensures as Special Education Administrator, Principal, Moderate Disabilities Teacher, and Elementary Education Teacher.

Other Eye On Education Books
Available From Routledge
(www.routledge.com/k-12)

Creating Inclusive Writing Environments in the K-12 Classroom: Reluctance, Resistance, and Strategies that Make a Difference
Angela Stockman

The Middle School Grammar Toolkit: Using Mentor Texts to Teach Standards-Based Language and Grammar in Grades 6–8, Second Edition
Sean Ruday

Sexuality for All Abilities: Teaching and Discussing Sexual Health in Special Education
Katie Thune and Molly Gage

Coding as a Playground: Programming and Computational Thinking in the Early Childhood Classroom, Second Edition
Marina Umaschi Bers

Implementing Project Based Learning in Early Childhood: Overcoming Misconceptions and Reaching Success
Sara Lev, Amanda Clark, and Erin Starkey

Grit, Resilience, and Motivation in Early Childhood: Practical Takeaways for Teachers
Lisa B. Fiore

Remote Learning Strategies for Students with IEPs

An Educator's Guidebook

Kathryn A. Welby

NEW YORK AND LONDON

First published 2021
by Routledge
605 Third Avenue, New York, NY 10158

and by Routledge
2 Park Square, Milton Park, Abingdon, Oxon, OX14 4RN

Routledge is an imprint of the Taylor & Francis Group, an informa business

© 2021 Kathryn A. Welby

The right of Kathryn A. Welby to be identified as author of this work has been asserted by her in accordance with sections 77 and 78 of the Copyright, Designs and Patents Act 1988.

All rights reserved. No part of this book may be reprinted or reproduced or utilised in any form or by any electronic, mechanical, or other means, now known or hereafter invented, including photocopying and recording, or in any information storage or retrieval system, without permission in writing from the publishers.

Trademark notice: Product or corporate names may be trademarks or registered trademarks, and are used only for identification and explanation without intent to infringe.

Library of Congress Cataloging-in-Publication Data
A catalog record for this book has been requested

ISBN: 978-0-367-75162-3 (hbk)
ISBN: 978-0-367-74150-1 (pbk)
ISBN: 978-1-003-16126-4 (ebk)

Typeset in Optima
by Apex CoVantage, LLC

Dedicated to Jack, Molly, and Megan

You three are my world!

XO

Contents

Acknowledgments viii

1 Introduction 1

2 Remote Learning and Special Education:
  The Challenge and the Research 11

3 Relationship Building 21

4 Parent/Caregiver Engagement 32

5 The Remote IEP Meeting 48

6 Remote Accommodations and Assistive Technology 67

7 Synchronous Activities and Strategies 81

8 Asynchronous Activities and Strategies 99

9 Paraprofessionals and Remote Learning 112

10 Tips and Tools to Share With Parents 126

11 Conclusion: Bringing It All Together 147

Acknowledgments

I want to acknowledge all of the amazing educators who participated and contributed to this project. Thank you!

I want to give special thanks to my editor, Eric Heckerson, and his remarkable ability to edit my writing and flow of thoughts. I am incredibly grateful for your attention to detail.

Thank you to my sister and photographer, Alyssa Rodrigues. Not only did you provide some great shots, but your listening ear, time, and feedback were valuable and always appreciated! Your participation makes everything fun!

My parents, Joanne and Charlie Cote, you are my role models, my strength, and my comfort. Thank you for always believing in me!

And a huge thank you to Tom, my husband, my inspiration. Having your support gives me the confidence to take risks beyond my comfort zone. Thank you for your continuous and ongoing encouragement!

1

Introduction

> *The most valuable resource that all educators have is each other. Without collaboration, our growth is limited to our own perspectives.*
> – Robert John Meehan

Parents, educators, administrators, and children across the country are struggling to keep up, barely keeping their heads above water. The challenges of remote special education are intense, the demands are high, and the specifics on the "how" are blurry. As I recently read on a billboard, "being part of history is exhausting!" and I could not agree more! The purpose of this guidebook is not to sugarcoat the reality of the struggle but to combine and share successes that have emerged from the struggle. As we experience this new chapter of educational history, we need to think beyond the textbook and beyond the schoolhouse walls because I can predict confidently that textbooks and possibly the schoolhouse itself are changing and, perhaps, slowly fading away. The notion that education can only happen in schools is no longer valid – learning can happen anywhere.

Purpose

The media, published surveys, and chatter throughout the schools continuously report a mountain of challenges related to remotely teaching children requiring special education services, but what about the success stories? Countless educators across the country are utilizing strategies that are effective and working well for them. It is time their voices are heard, and their success is shared to help our colleagues who continue to face challenges. This book and the motivation behind the research provide an optimistic approach to address some of the undeniable difficulties of remote learning, particularly for children with learning challenges and disabilities.

Specifically, this book aims to improve remote learning for students with Individualized Education Programs (IEPs). Use this book as a guide or reference when planning activities and communications for your remote classroom. Pick and choose from the variety of suggestions offered throughout each chapter. When teaching children with various learning needs and challenges, we must acknowledge that every child is different, and each child's needs are different. What works for one child may not work for another; therefore, an assortment of ideas and tools are shared from diverse educators' perspectives working in very different geographic locations throughout the country.

In combination with research and practice, this book was created to provide educators with practical and useful strategies to improve remote learning for students with IEPs that can be utilized immediately. This guidebook is packed with ideas, techniques, resources, and success stories to read and keep handy as a reference when planning and teaching your remote classroom. Teaching academics and providing services such as physical therapy, occupational therapy, and speech and language to children who receive special education services remotely can be challenging. This book will address the complexity of the challenges and offer suggestions to:

1. Build relationships and community with students in the remote classroom.
2. Increase parent engagement in a remote setting.
3. Conduct a virtual IEP meeting.
4. Convert IEP accommodations to the remote classroom.
5. Develop practical synchronous teaching activities.

6. Develop effective asynchronous teaching activities.
7. Utilize paraprofessionals in the remote classroom.
8. Provide parents with suggestions and tips to help their children independently succeed at home.

While there is still a great deal to learn on how to address all learners' needs remotely, suggestions to these and many other remote obstacles are answered throughout the guidebook. The strategies are a foundation of knowledge upon which you can build and learn.

Background

As a consequence of the global pandemic, tens of millions of students experienced a dramatic switch in how their education was delivered, from in-person, in-school delivery to remote, home-based learning. As the coronavirus began spreading across the United States, education as we know it changed abruptly.

A few weeks after the school's sudden closure, educators, parents, and others started asking for help on how to teach children with special education needs remotely. I could have provided a theoretical perspective on what *should* work based on special education learning theories and my knowledge as a special education teacher and professor. Still, I was far from an expert at the novel practice of teaching children with disabilities remotely. In my opinion, the theory is important, but the practice and experiences are even more important when working with children diagnosed with a variety of disabilities and learning challenges. What works for one child may not work for another child, even with the same diagnosis and medical makeup. As Dr. Stephen Shore famously stated, "if you've met one person diagnosed with autism, you've met one person diagnosed with autism". I learned quickly that the statement holds true for all diagnosed disabilities and learning challenges. Successfully teaching children who require special education services is not only a science but an art that relies heavily on trial and error, reflection, and purposeful relationship development. To learn effective strategies for teaching children with special education needs remotely, I turned to the many outstanding and experienced teachers, administrators, and service providers in the field that are working with children with IEPs.

In April 2020, I reached out to a few colleagues with a quick survey, and they shared the survey with other effective educators. Within a week, over 90 teachers throughout the Northeast contributed success stories teaching students with IEPs in a remote environment. Using the information collected from the educators throughout the Northeast, I combined and shared the results through virtual professional development to help teachers finish off the 2019–2020 school year.

Unfortunately, back to school 2020 and education did not resume to a standard in-person approach. Tens of millions of students began the school year completely remote, including 13 of the 15 largest school districts in the US. Many other school districts adopted a hybrid or blended learning model that included a mix of remote learning and in-person learning. The main concern cited was safety for staff and students. As many school districts continued with full or partial remote education, the expectations for educators amplified.

Given the greater expectations for academic and service delivery combined with the continued challenges of educating students with disabilities and learning challenges remotely, I decided to formalize the research. I expanded this project with outreach to educators across the US to share successful strategies and tools. Luckily, I collected hundreds of strategies from over 250 educators across the country. I also used my prior knowledge and experiences as a special education teacher to add approaches and recommendations for converting IEP accommodations and assistive technology into remote practice. With the hundreds of collected strategies and in a combination of practice, this book was created to provide educators with practical and useful strategies to improve remote learning for students with IEPs.

Eventually, the 2020 pandemic will be a distant memory, but the educational landscape will most likely forever change. By building more opportunities for remote learning options designed for all learners, including students who receive special education services, we as educators must prepare for the future. Like many others, I predict that remote learning will be a part of education's future going forward. Together, we are experiencing history.

Who Would Benefit From Reading This Guidebook?

The intended audience is preschool through high school educators working remotely with students with learning challenges and disabilities. Specifically, all educators who work remotely with children on IEPs would benefit from the strategies in this guidebook, such as:

- Teachers (all types).
- Administrators.
- Paraprofessionals.
- Occupational therapists.
- Physical therapists.
- Speech and language pathologists.
- School counselors.
- Behaviors specialists.
- Tutors.
- Teacher preparation students.
- All other outside service providers.

Parents of children with IEPs could also benefit from learning the content outlined in the chapters. In a nutshell, the intended audience is all educators and parents working remotely with children with learning challenges and disabilities. Most strategies outlined in this guidebook could be used for all learners at all ability levels.

The Structure of the Book

Each chapter contains a brief yet relevant introduction of the topic then dives into the research, remote strategies, success stories, quick tips from educators, highlighted resources, and a summary of important points brought up within the chapter. The goal is for an easy reading guidebook with quick references to refer to and manage your remote instruction for students with IEPs.

Chapter 2 – Remote Learning and Special Education: The Challenge and the Research

As a consequence of the global pandemic of 2020, tens of millions of students experienced their education come to a rapid halt. As coronavirus began spreading across the US, the educational landscape changed, and it changed quickly. With the sudden shift to remote learning, educators across the country faced a massive dilemma of changing decades of teaching and learning seemingly overnight. The interruption in learning has been incredibly hard on students with Individualized Education Programs (IEPs). Media and research report that the switch has been difficult for parents and school districts across the country, yet according to the author's recently distributed survey, educators feel that they have successfully taught children with IEPs remotely. Chapter 2 is the book's foundation, highlighting the challenges of remote learning, an overview of the author's collected research, and a snapshot of results. By examining the Individuals with Disabilities Education Act (IDEA) and its application to the remote environment in parallel with the challenges of remote learning, the purpose of the research is to improve remote education for students with IEPs.

Chapter 3 – Relationship Building

Developing and establishing relationships between educators and students is an essential first step in creating a remote classroom. The power of relationships builds trust, creates a feeling of belonging, and can increase achievement and learning. In educational settings, research suggests that positive and established student-teacher relationships can foster student engagement, influence motivation, increase participation, and improve student achievement. Chapter 3 emphasizes the importance of relationship building and provides strategies to build and strengthen relationships remotely. Educators across the country share strategies that have worked in their remote classrooms. Many of these strategies can be used for students of all ability levels.

Chapter 4 – Parent/Caregiver Engagement

For a successful remote learning experience for children with learning challenges and disabilities, parent engagement is crucial. Involvement, mutual decision making, collaboration, and ongoing communication are essential for the child's success. Parents and educators should work as a coordinated, supportive team to create a home school partnership built around the child's success. Chapter 4 intends to share successful strategies to encourage parent engagement and partnerships to add to a sense of stability and consistency in the unpredictable world of remote learning.

Chapter 5 – The Remote IEP Meeting

As a result of the global pandemic of 2020, school shutdowns forced IEP meetings to take place remotely. The virtual IEP meeting started as a temporary solution to the inability to meet in person. However, educators have noted the benefits of the remote IEP meeting, and some predict remote sessions could turn into the preferred choice for team meetings well into the future. Educators report, through survey results with follow-up interviews, ideas and best practices for successful remote IEP meetings. A collection of district-wide forms, agendas, and meeting norms were collected to understand useful and practical strategies to carry out the remote IEP meeting, from pre-meeting preparation through post-meeting signatures. The remote IEP meeting can be as effective as in-person meetings with proper logistical and personal preparation. Establishing roles, creating effective privacy practices, instituting norms, access to technology, and following an agenda can ensure successful implementation of the remote IEP meeting.

Chapter 6 – Remote Accommodations and Assistive Technology

Accommodations and assistive technology are essential and required in the remote learning environment for students with IEPs. The challenge is effectively transferring the accommodations from in-person learning to the remote classroom. Chapter 6 demonstrates that many accommodations can be replicated at home through educational technology, virtual applications, available household items, or various assistive technology options. Grouped by presentation, setting, response, and scheduling, the most frequently used in-person IEP accommodations are explored and reproduced for remote learning.

Chapter 7 – Synchronous Activities and Strategies
After years of teaching, earning multiple degrees, and incorporating professional development hours, many educators would soon need to learn how to teach children with diagnosed disabilities – in real-time, over the Internet – and they must do so while continuing to adhere to all the IDEA laws, to reinforce IEP goals and objectives, and to provide appropriate accommodations. A collection of synchronous strategies to engage children with disabilities and learning challenges are shared in Chapter 7. The strategies communicated in this chapter are a collection of successful approaches by educators who, in 2020, had to quickly pivot their teaching to the remote learning classroom with little training or guidance. Through trial and error, the dedicated educators working with students with IEPs share their victories. Of course, every child is different, and what works for one may not work for another, but this collection of ideas and approaches should supply a foundation of tricks and tools to attempt.

Chapter 8 – Asynchronous Activities and Strategies
Some might think that creating independent asynchronous learning activities for students with learning challenges is an impossible feat, but outstanding educators across the country are proving the skeptics wrong. Through initial student coaching, parent support, and proper preparation, educators are making it happen – and surpassing expectations. Educators have found strategies to keep students with IEPs on task and achieve IEP goals with minimal teacher intervention during scheduled asynchronous learning time. Asynchronous learning is a collaborative and interactive learning community not limited by a time and place because it does not live in real-time. Typically, students attend to their learning on their own, with shared resources from an instructor. A compilation of asynchronous strategies to engage children with disabilities and

learning challenges is shared in Chapter 8. The methods communicated in this chapter are a collection of successful approaches by educators. Through trial and error, the dedicated educators working with students with IEPs share their asynchronous victories.

Chapter 9 – Paraprofessionals and Remote Learning

The paraprofessional's role is essential to a special education classroom's success, and most teachers would be lost without them. Paraprofessionals typically have a hands-on role with students with IEPs throughout the day and focus on support in the classroom, during services such as occupational therapy, physical therapy, and speech and language therapy; recess activities; and unified arts. There are many ways the paraprofessional can and should continue to provide support to students, teachers, and programs when schools transition to remote learning. Supporting the teacher throughout the transition to remote is critical in the consistency of the programming and students' success with IEPs. Chapter 9 provides suggestions and strategies to include the paraprofessional in remote tasks and assisting.

Chapter 10 – Tips and Tools to Share With Parents

As a result of the 2020 global pandemic, caregivers who have children with learning challenges, variously diagnosed disabilities, and exceptionalities have been asked to do the nearly impossible – teach their children while maintaining their home, multiple children's schooling, and their employment responsibilities. Parents are concerned about the logistics of the task and the fear of their children falling behind academically and missing developmental milestones while losing the life skills necessary for independent living. Throughout the guidebook, strategies are shared for educators to improve remote learning for students with IEPs, and many of the shared strategies can apply to the home. Chapter 10 highlights those helpful home strategies for parents that were mentioned throughout the book and provides some resources for caregiver support. Additionally, Chapter 10 will explore a parent's perspective, some available research and survey results, and tricks and tools educators can share with parents.

Chapter 11 – Conclusion: Bringing It All Together

The progression of educating children with disabilities and learning challenges in a remote environment is an area for continuous improvement and further exploration. Ongoing research and continued development will be necessary to successfully implement remote learning for students with Individualized Education Programs (IEPs), especially as the educational landscape continues to change, offering more opportunities for remote learning. Successfully teaching children who require special education relies heavily on trial and error, reflection, and purposeful relationship development. All of these strategies provided and shared by educators are wonderful and should be individualized to meet each student's specific educational and emotional needs. Furthermore, four distinct generalizations emerged that can be takeaways for all remote special education programs. In the calibration of survey results, interviews, and document gathering, the overarching suggestions for a successful foundation for remote instruction for students with IEPs yielded the development of four significant findings: the importance of relationships, parent engagement, communications, and consistent structures.

Author's Note: All 257 participants provided a signed consent to participate in the study. Some tips were shared anonymously with location only and some of the names have been changed throughout the chapters to preserve anonymity.

2

Remote Learning and Special Education: The Challenge and the Research

> *We are experiencing history, an exciting change in education. As educators, we expand our practice and grow because the standards and expectations are so high. We are implementing various instructional styles to accommodate all learners and abilities while using technological resources, pulling student groups in different formats, communicating in different ways, co-teaching with service providers, and integrating more engaging materials. The year of the pivot, 2020, proved that the school's brick and mortar concept is archaic.*
>
> – Adam Mullen, Second Grade Inclusion Teacher

As a consequence of the global pandemic, in March 2020, tens of millions of students saw their education come to a rapid halt. As coronavirus began spreading across the United States, the educational landscape changed, and it changed quickly. Administrators teaming up with educators started to scramble to create a remote curriculum seemingly overnight and with very little time to prepare. Suddenly, school districts worldwide had to redesign lesson plans and change educational objectives with minimal training and remote teaching background. Interrupted education has been incredibly hard on students with Individualized Education Programs (IEPs).

As educators, we recognize that the foundation of a successful special education program is built around structure and routine. Suddenly routine and structure were diminished entirely. Remote, hybrid, and blended learning typically lack the typical structure and routine established in the schools.

According to the U.S. Department of Education, National Center for Education Statistics (NCES), approximately seven million students have learning challenges, diagnosed disabilities, and exceptionalities that qualify them to receive special education services under the Individuals with Disabilities Education Act (IDEA). Specifically, according to NCES (2020), 14 percent of the total number of children in public schools qualified for an IEP, an individualized special education program designed to meet students' specific learning needs. According to IDEA (2004), an IEP is a written document developed by a team of individuals, including educators, service providers, outside service providers, and caregivers, that lists the services, accommodations, and annual goals that the students will receive.

Two of the primary purposes of the IEP are to set reasonable learning goals for the students and list the services the school district will provide for them. Under IDEA, public schools must provide students with free and appropriate public education regardless of various abilities, disabilities, and learning challenges. With the quick switch to remote learning, educators were challenged to educate seven million children with IEPs focusing on meeting their learning goals and continue to provide other essential support such as, and not limited to, speech, occupational, and physical therapy.

Providing students who require special education services an appropriate and effective remote education has proven to be challenging for everyone involved, including teachers, parents, administrators, service providers, and most importantly, the child. There has been minimal training and research on evidence-based strategies to teach children with IEPs remotely. Before 2020, we can assume that teacher preparation programs were not providing courses on teaching children with disabilities remotely. Furthermore, teacher in-service professional development days were not spent developing remote curriculum for children with IEPs. Unfortunately, in a field of continuous professional development, most educators had received no training on how to educate students remotely with IEPs. Educators had to start from scratch and learn through trial and error.

With the sudden remote shift, we as educators were faced with a daunting task – dramatically changing decades of teaching and learning, as well as determining how to accommodate some of the most vulnerable learners in a remote environment. Meanwhile, we were all faced with learning the various options and logistics for effectively teaching students remotely.

To adjust to new ideas and face the most recent educational challenge of change seemed like an incredible feat that educators across the country were expected to handle with poise. How will educators adhere to IDEA expectations and meet the individualized needs of so many children while teaching remotely?

IDEA

Enacted in 1975, IDEA, formerly known as the Education for All Handicapped Children Act, requires that all children, regardless of disabilities and learning challenges, are entitled to a free and appropriate public education. The law does not waiver given any circumstances, including a global pandemic. On April 27, 2020, US Secretary of Education Betsy DeVos clarified that although school buildings were physically closed, creating significant challenges to the special education community, she would not recommend or approve any waivers that would affect or lessen the requirements of IDEA. Students were expected to receive the same level of services and academics outlined in a child's IEP without any clarity or guidance for educators on *how* to do so.

Remote Education and Challenges

Educators across the country immediately set out to address the challenges confronting them and explore their options. Researchers sought to understand how school closures would affect school districts, parents, and students. They began to survey key stakeholders to collect data and insight into these challenges.

One survey was conducted through the American Institutes for Research (AIR). The study, called *The National Survey of the Public*

Education's Response to COVID-19, was distributed to understand how the forced school closures of 2020 affected school districts' ability to implement appropriate instruction and practices for students with disabilities. According to Jackson and Bowdon (2020), participating school districts reported that complying with IDEA was extremely challenging during remote instruction. Of the 744 responses from school districts, over 70 percent of the districts reported that it was more difficult to provide needed accommodations and specifically designed instruction remotely to students who require additional support. Additionally, over 60 percent of the school districts reported providing services such as speech therapy was more challenging during remote instruction. More than half said that collaborating with social services and outside agencies was more difficult while participating in remote education. Consequently, most school districts reported that it was more challenging to engage with parents and caregivers for help with IEP requirements. Overall, the survey found that educators experienced tremendous roadblocks and challenges while teaching children who require special education services remotely.

In addition to AIR's research, families also acknowledge the struggle of teaching children remotely while adhering to IDEA and IEP requirements. For example, Echelon Insights conducted a coronavirus family impact survey weekly of 500 parents of public school students from April 27, 2020, through May 20, 2020. Over 60 percent of families believe schools should focus on rethinking the best way to educate students, and districts should develop new teaching methods (American Enterprise Institute, 2020).

Another survey of parents through ConnectEd (2020) reported similar findings. The 2,234 Washington, D.C., parents were asked questions regarding the impact of remote learning on their child's education. The results show that parents are struggling and are overwhelmed with all of the typical remote learning challenges. Unfortunately, 73 percent of families with children with IEPs think their children will not receive some or all appropriate services.

The findings are parallel to media reports around the country. Journalists have provided awareness from the viewpoints of parents who have been upset with the assumed lack of compliance with IDEA requirements, IEP accommodations, and learning plans for their children with disabilities (DiSalvo, 2020; Hays, 2020; Stein & Strauss, 2020). With the perception that their children are not receiving the services outlined in the IEP, parents across the country are upset and struggling to provide their children with everything they need while engaged in remote instruction.

Survey findings, media coverage, parents, educators, service providers, and school districts all report an intense struggle and challenge with educating children who require special education services remotely. The depth of the problem stretches way beyond the school district; this is a global challenge.

Since there is an abundance of research on the challenges and roadblocks of teaching children with disabilities and learning challenges remotely, I decided to research and find those success stories to provide educators with tips and tools to improve the overall remote instruction experience. Luckily, 257 educators from four countries and 37 states across the US were willing to share their success stories and successful practices. My study sought to combine successful techniques to share and disseminate to help educators navigate the challenging educational landscape and improve remote education for children with disabilities and learning challenges.

My Research

The approaches outlined in each chapter are a collection of successful remote instruction strategies used in teaching children from pre-kindergarten through twelfth grade with disabilities and learning challenges. The methods are reported from a diverse group of educators.

Participants

The research includes results and strategies from 257 contributing educators from across 37 states in the US and four countries.

Data were collected through a questionnaire. Known educators working with children with learning challenges and disabilities were asked to participate and share the survey with colleagues who are successfully working with children who receive special education services. The survey was also posted on social media sites in specific closed educator groups such as the American Educational Research Association (AERA), Global Educator Collective, and Merrimack College Institute for New Teacher Support (MINTS). Lastly, random sampling was done through email outreach to administrators and educational leaders across the US.

The survey was open for participation from October 20, 2020, through November 12, 2020, and remained open until saturation was accomplished, and no new themes or ideas emerged within the survey results.

The results also yield 58 educators who volunteered for a follow-up interview. Based on survey results, district size, and diversity of positions, 12 participants were chosen for a follow-up interview. The interview elaborated on survey results and investigated the virtual IEP meeting. Additionally, after to speaking to individuals, documents and tutorials regarding the virtual IEP meeting, special education remote learning updates, and online tutorials were collected and analyzed from school districts throughout the country. The following is a list of the survey participants:

- Special education teachers.
- General education teachers.
- Administrators.
- Paraprofessionals.
- Support personnel/counselors.
- Intervention specialists.
- Teachers of the deaf.
- Music teachers.
- Library specialists.
- Physical education teachers/adaptive physical education teachers.
- Autism specialists.
- Reading specialists.
- Assessment consultants.
- Behavior specialists.
- Intervention specialists.
- English language learner teachers.

- ♦ Registered behavior technicians.
- ♦ Vocational coordinators.
- ♦ Physical therapists.
- ♦ Occupational therapists.
- ♦ Speech and language pathologists.

The majority of the participants worked with students who would be considered within the moderate disability range. Specifically, 83 percent worked remotely with children on IEPs that would be considered in the moderate disability range and typically learn in the inclusion classroom, resource room, co-taught classroom, and general education classroom. Additionally, 17 percent of the participants worked with students in more intense needs or medically fragile populations located in substantially separate classrooms or outside placements, such as collaboratives.

Looking at the breakdown of age and grade level, most educators who participated worked with elementary-aged children. Here is the breakdown by grade:

- ♦ 6 percent of the educators worked with pre-K students.
- ♦ 57 percent of the educators worked with children, grades K–5.
- ♦ 13 percent of the educators worked with middle school students, grades 6–8.
- ♦ 23 percent of the educators worked with high school students, grades 9–12.

In a combination of the demographics, most contributors were K–8 teachers who resided in the US. Most participating educators work with students diagnosed with moderate disabilities who learn in their least restrictive environments, with same-age peers in the general education setting for the majority of the day.

Results

In addition to collecting strategies and ideas that will be shared throughout the next chapters, I wanted to get a sense of how most educators felt about teaching children with learning challenges and disabilities remotely.

Using a Likert scale, with five options strongly agree, somewhat agree, neither agree nor disagree, somewhat disagree, and strongly disagree, the results show that:

- 59 percent of educators strongly agree/somewhat agree that they are successfully working remotely with students with IEPs.
- 51 percent of educators strongly agree/somewhat agree that parents have been engaged in remote learning.
- 31 percent of educators strongly agree/somewhat agree that their school district has provided professional development or instruction on how to provide remote education for children on IEPs.
- 63 percent of educators strongly agree/somewhat agree that students with IEPs have been successful at remote learning.
- 86 percent of educators strongly agree/somewhat agree that they are confident in their ability to teach children with IEPs remotely.

Most of the participating educators feel confident in their abilities to teach children with IEPs remotely. There was a split on parent engagement. Approximately half of the participants felt that parents are engaged, while the other half felt that parent engagement had room for improvement.

An alarming finding was only 31 percent of the participating educators' school districts provided training or professional development on teaching children with IEPs. Consequently, 69 percent of educators have not been provided training or professional development to teach children with IEPs remotely.

Overall Themes

In addition to the previously mentioned data collection, the survey asked open-ended questions, including the following:

- Participating educators were asked to share successful strategies teaching students with IEPs remotely.
- Participating educators were asked about successful strategies promoting parent engagement in the remote learning environment.

- Participating educators were asked to share successful strategies utilizing paraprofessional while remote teaching.
- Participating educators were asked recommendations for remote assistive technology.
- Participating educators were asked to add any remote learning success story that could help other educators.

Unexpected responses included many mentions of the virtual IEP meetings and proved that was an area I needed to further research. Therefore, 12 administrators, teachers, and service providers who participate in remote IEP meetings were called for follow-up interviews to understand how to conduct successful remote IEP meetings. Additionally, district-wide professional development documents, online tutorials, IEP meeting agendas, and IEP participation guidelines were collected and analyzed to understand how to implement a successful virtual IEP meeting.

The survey and interview results were coded, and themes surfaced. Each chapter will discuss the themes and depth of the findings and highlight educator success stories and tips.

The unforgettable year of 2020 led to an abrupt switch to remote learning, and the educational landscape changed quickly. The switch has been incredibly hard on students with IEPs. Media and research report that the switch has been difficult for parents and school districts across the country, yet according to my recently distributed survey, more than half of the educators feel that they have successfully taught children with IEPs remotely. The successes should be captured and shared! In the next few chapters, the strategies collected within the survey results will be communicated to help those working with children with IEPs.

References

American Enterprise Institute. (2020). *Coronavirus family impact survey.* Washington, DC: American Enterprise Institute.

ConnectEd. (2020). *Covid-19 parent survey results.* Washington, DC. Retrieved from http://dcschoolreform.org/sites/default/files/ConnectED%20Parent%20Survey%20Results_1.pdf

DiSalvo, E. (2020, July 27). Parents: Distance learning a "disaster" for kids with disabilities. *CTPost*. Retrieved from www.ctpost.com/news/coronavirus/article/Parents-Distance-learning-a-disaster-for-15436646.php

Hays, E. (2020, September 11). Special Ed parents: Remote school fails. *New Haven Independent*. Retrieved from www.newhavenindependent.org/index.php/archives/entry/special_education_remote_school

Individuals with Disabilities Education Act. (2004). https://sites.ed.gov/idea/

Jackson, D., & Bowdon, J. (2020). *Spotlight on students with disabilities*. National Survey of Public Education's Response to COVID-19. American Institutes for Research. Retrieved from www.air.org/sites/default/files/COVID-Survey-Spotlight-on-Students-with-Disabilities-FINAL-Oct-2020.pdf

Stein, P., & Strauss, V. (2020, August 7). Special education students are not just falling behind in the pandemic – They're losing key skills, parents say. *The Washington Post*. Retrieved from www.washingtonpost.com/local/education/special-education-students-are-not-just-falling-behind-theyre-losing-key-skills-parents-say/2020/08/05/ec1b91ca-cffd-11ea-9038-af089b63ac21_story.html

U.S. Department of Education, Institute of Education Sciences, National Center for Education Statistics. (2020). *The condition of education: Students with disabilities*. Retrieved from https://nces.ed.gov/programs/coe/indicator_cgg.asp

3

Relationship Building

Remote teaching has been an overall success. It has been great getting to know our students better. Our relationship is even closer now than it was in person. They have all met my dog, noticed that I have an awkward number of house plants and that I drink way too much coffee. I also met their dog, see their families regularly, and notice that they drink Mountain Dew for breakfast!
  – Sheri Mistretta, High School Special Education Vocational Coordinator

Developing and establishing a relationship with your students is, first and foremost, the most important step to take when creating your remote learning environment. The power of relationship building builds trust within your classroom, generates a feeling of belonging, and in turn, can increase achievement and learning. Students want to connect with you, and they want to know you!

Looking back at their days of remote instruction, students will probably not remember the math lesson you spent three hours creating in hopes that they learn long division. But they will remember the day you called them personally when you suspected they had a tough day. They will remember the silly hats you wore because you wanted to see them smile. They will remember the funny story you told them about your cat eating all the birdseed from your bird feeder. They will remember that you had faith in their abilities. They will remember your kind words of encouragement when they struggled. They will remember *you* and the way you made them feel. The relationship you establish will your students is the foundation of a successful remote classroom.

The approaches outlined in this chapter are all-inclusive strategies applied to the remote learning classroom, regardless of ability and disabilities. This chapter focuses on establishing a foundation for building a strong relationship with your remote-learning students. Regardless of ability or the diagnosis of a disability, a positive educator-student relationship is the foundation of a successful year.

In educational settings, research suggests that positive and established student and teacher relationships can foster student engagement, influence motivation, increase participation, and improve student achievement (Cook et al., 2018; Cornelius-White, 2007; Hughes & Cao, 2017; Lee, 2012; Vollet, Kindermann, & Skinner, 2017). Positive student-teacher relationships include mutual respect, open communication, warmth, and affection. Specifically, research proves that positive student-teacher relationships increase participation in the classroom setting and have resulted in a greater interest in school for all students, with and without learning challenges and behavioral difficulties (Birch & Ladd, 1997; Tsai & Cheney, 2012). The same classroom research and strategies apply in a remote setting.

Developing a relationship with students builds academic success in a positive learning environment, shapes a classroom community, creates a student's self-worth, and minimizes behavioral challenges. As educators, the importance of relationship building with students is reinforced throughout teacher preparation programs, department meetings, and professional development activities. Small gestures, such as standing at the door while students enter with a smile and high five, can change the day. Remote learning thrives on engagement, and engagement can be achieved and improve through relationship building.

The Research

Throughout the various surveys of educators, relationship building was a reoccurring theme. The responses suggest that time spent building relationships improves the effectiveness of remote learning. When asked to share a successful remote teaching strategy, many participants pointed to a relationship-building theme or component such as sending an email, working one-on-one, constant communication, home deliveries, check-in parades, mailing items home, sending notes, engaging in games, check-in times, having fun together, and sending occasional text messages. Research and interview results both suggested several reoccurring strategies found to be effective, outlined in the following sections.

Distance Learning Relationship-Building Strategies

How can we apply relationship-building strategies to the distance learning model? The following techniques can be used with students who exhibit various ability levels and can be modified depending on their cognitive ability and individualized needs. Here are some successful strategies shared:

One-on-One Virtual Meeting
Start the year with a virtual one-on-one meeting with each student. Act as if it is a semi-structured interview and have a set of questions to learn more about each student while leaving time for probing questions. In this meeting, find one mutual interest where you can connect with and expand the discussion. Here are ten sample questions to explore with your students:

1. What is your favorite activity to do when not in school?
2. If you could live anywhere in the world, where would it be?
3. What makes you happy?
4. What makes you angry?
5. What would you change about yourself if you could?
6. What motivates you to work hard?
7. What is your proudest accomplishment?
8. What makes you laugh the most?
9. If you could choose to do anything for a day, what would it be?
10. If you could only eat one meal for the rest of your life, what would it be?

Student Check-Ins
With the remote learning model, educators will need to create continuous opportunities to check in with students. The excitement of the new school year can wear off quickly, and students may get lost or fall behind. Knowing that there are continued check-ins would promote student accountability and provide a chance for you to reconnect with your students.

Student Letters, Surveys, and Questionnaires
As an alternative to one-on-one check-ins, start the school year off by sending each student a questionnaire or survey using Google Forms (as an example) to better understand your students. You can ask the same questions you would on a one-to-one meeting. Use the questionnaires' results throughout the year to reconnect with students and reference when meeting with them and their parents.

Solicit Parent Input
In addition to starting the year with your students' meeting, meet with your students' parents. Investing time at the beginning of the year to meet with parents will help you get to know your students. Parent meetings can create alliancing and partnerships with a mutual intent to promote student success.

Classroom Google Slide of Interests, Family, Talents
At the beginning of the school year, create a classroom "all about us" slideshow. Have each student decorate a slide with pictures, words, phrases all about them. Show the slides one by one to the class to foster relationship building among students. Highlight students' similarities and differences through a class activity. Additionally, the educator has access to those slides throughout the year and can refer to them in a pinch to connect or view before meeting with a student.

Send Them Mail
Throughout the year, send a quick card or note to tell students you are thinking about them, you are proud of them, noticed an

increase in effort, saw they are working hard, or maybe you are proud of their grit. Be specific to the student. Even if the letter is only a line or two, you show them you take an interest in their well-being. Mailing them a quick card, message, or note shows them you care.

Daily Hello Video

Record and post or send a daily hello video to the class. In this video, tell students something that happened to you or something that made you happy, sad, disappointed, scared, etc. Show your feelings and tell them something new, so they get to know you a little better.

Zoom Waiting Room

Have students log in and wait in a virtual "waiting room" at the start of a virtual class so you can greet each of them one at a time by name. The "waiting room" is available through online platforms, such as Zoom. The idea mirrors the concept of standing at the classroom entrance, saying hello to each student. Waiting rooms may take a bit longer than greeting each student at the door, but educators report that it is worth the time.

Mental Health Morning Meetings

As part of morning meetings, consider pausing academics by starting with meditations, resilience training, discussions of gratefulness, thoughts of growth mindset, and other lively conversations that can make a student's day a bit brighter. Several teachers reported that spending five to ten minutes a day on mental well-being had made a positive difference for themselves and many students. The benefits have paid off in other ways, such as increased engagement, participation, and improved attendance. Educators feel that students show up and look forward to the positive mental health morning meetings.

Close the Gap Between Special Education and General Education

Special education teachers recommend that general education teachers spend extra time getting to know the students in their class with IEPs; therefore, the general education teacher will not need to rely on case managers and special educators to bridge the relationship. It will pay off in the long term by investing the time at the beginning of the year.

Emoji Share
Have students select an emoji a day to describe their mood. Emoji mood shares can be executed as a private chat on platforms such as Zoom, email outreach, or a Google Form. You can start the day or remote learning session with a private emoji mood share. The mood shared could help guide your lesson or your daily objective and inform which students may need support and attention.

Mini-Me Avatars
Create a mini-me avatar using an app such as Bitmoji. Have your students also create a Bitmoji. Educators are using an avatar to create a fun way to connect with students. Without being present, educators can share their moods and feelings virtually.

Let Students Inside Your World
Educators sometimes get so wrapped in the lesson objectives; they forget to take time and let students get to know them. You can let them in by sharing stories about your family and your pets. Share stories with students about your struggles with completing work, staying on task, paying attention, or staying organized. Stories that do not have a perfect result can be beneficial. They show how, even as the teacher or educator, you have to keep problem-solving to find strategies that work.

Give Students a Voice
Have students create virtual rules and expectations to follow, promoting classroom community and accountability. Research suggests that students who believe they have a voice in school are much more likely to be academically motivated than students who do not think they have a voice. Involving students in classroom decision making increases their engagement and encourages their

growth (Quaglia & Corso, 2014). The theory of student's voice can and should apply to remote learning. Create a virtual learning environment that allows students to participate in decision making and expectations.

Understand Student Needs

Ask the students what they need to be successful while remote learning. More specifically, ask for their help as you try to understand their needs. This strategy is useful for connecting because you share ownership in their success and establish that both of you are responsible for working together to make sure that the student's needs are met. In the conversations, be clear about your objectives while considering what the student needs to learn. This process not only shows students that you respect and value their ideas and thoughts, but it can also give you some useful information in creating your online curriculum.

Apply Classroom Relationship-Building Strategies to the Virtual Classroom

Use the same baseline relationship-building techniques in the remote classroom setting as you would in the classroom. These include the following:

- Use students' names when you talk to them or call on them.
- Actively listen to their stories.
- Acknowledge all responses and questions.
- Build on what you learn from students by sharing stories, interests, and worries.
- Understand students' expressions and look into the reasons behind their current mood.
- Paraphrase their message, when appropriate.

Virtual Office Hours

Hold virtual office hours once a week. The virtual hours can be an opportunity for students to talk regarding questions, concerns, and feedback and to share something that happened during their day.

The importance of relationship building is essential in the development of a successful remote classroom. Remember that your students want to know YOU and will remember the way you made them feel. To develop a relationship with the student, make time for personal connections by setting up one-on-one meetings. Individualized meetings show students that you care and value the relationship. Don't forget to offer the same level of respect in the remote classroom as you would in person, and most importantly, smile and have fun!

Success Story

Stephanie, a third-grade teacher in Massachusetts, adds some fun to build relationships with students.

At the beginning of the year, Stephanie meets with each of her students' parents. She asks them to give her two or three trivia-style questions about their child. She then creates a trivia game (remotely through Kahoot!), and all the students get to learn about each other through the trivia questions and answers provided by the parents. The students have a blast and get to know each other. The games are fun, build a positive classroom community, and improve the remote relationships between the students in her class and herself. This activity sets the tone for the school year, and she immediately gets to know her students. Stephanie also refers to the information provided to her through the parents in individual connections with students.

Quick Tips From Educators

Maria, a fifth-grade inclusion teacher from New Hampshire, recommends spending 15 minutes each morning working on a growth mindset that emphasizes courage, gratefulness, and forgiveness. She teaches her students how to work through stress by using brave breaths and relaxing their bodies. She uses a program called *Choose*

Love created by Scarlett Lewis. There is no cost to access the curriculum, and it is designed to teach students how to choose love in any circumstance creating a safe and connected school culture.

Michelle, a high school special education teacher from California, recommends constant communication. Michelle uses the *Remind App* to check in with students. The Remind App allows effective communication between teachers and students by sending messages directly to the student's phone as a text message. Since most high school students frequently use their phones, this app is a direct communication tool with her students without giving them her phone number.

Sheri, a high school special education vocational coordinator from Massachusetts, recommends being overly supportive and slowly building trust. She recommends superficial conversation starters by looking at the surrounding space captured through video conferencing. Using background visuals, ask questions to get to know your students, and slowly build from there. Sheri explained that many students could be closed off and unwilling to share. Still, if you start small without prying, you can eventually build strong connections. The questions can be as generic as I noticed a red couch in the background. Do you like the color red? Sometimes they can offer insights into their world, and you can ask clarifying questions to create a connection.

 Highlighted Resource

Understood.org has printable resources that promote partnerships with families and are available at no cost for educators to download and use in their remote classrooms. Understood.org has a series called *Back-to-School for Educators: Start With Relationships* that includes articles, printable, and other valuable resources. The web address is here:

> www.understood.org/en/school-learning/for-educators/partnering-with-families/printable-back-to-school-update-to-learn-from-families

Remember

- ✓ Relationships are important! The power of relationship building builds trust within your classroom, creates a feeling of belonging, and in turn, can increase achievement and learning.
- ✓ You can develop and establish a relationship with your students by collecting information about your students. Keep collected information as a reference to refer to all year.
- ✓ Follow in-person relationship-building strategies and apply them to the remote classroom, such as using students' names when you talk to them or call on them.
- ✓ Build a classroom community through opportunities to highlight similarities and differences among students.
- ✓ Make time to meet, talk, and connect one-on-one with students.
- ✓ Actively listen and build upon what students share with you.
- ✓ Students want to know all about YOU – share stories, interests, and worries.
- ✓ Students will remember how you made them feel and the extra time you invested in them.
- ✓ Smile and have fun!

References

Birch, S. H., & Ladd, G. W. (1997). The teacher–child relationship and children's early school adjustment. *Journal of School Psychology, 35*(1), 61–79. https://doi.org/10.1016/S0022-4405(96)00029-5

Cook, C. R., Fiat, A., Larson, M., Daikos, C., Slemrod, T., Holland, E. A., . . . & Renshaw, T. (2018). Positive greetings at the door: Evaluation of a low-cost, high-yield proactive classroom management strategy. *Journal of Positive Behavior Interventions, 20*(3), 149–159. https://doi.org/10.1177/1098300717753831

Cornelius-White, J. (2007). Learner-centered teacher-student relationships are effective: A meta-analysis. *Review of Educational Research, 77*, 113–143. https://doi.org/10.3102/003465430298563

Hughes, J., & Cao, Q. (2017). Trajectories of teacher-student warmth and conflict at the transition to middle school: Effects on academic engagement and achievement. *Journal of School Psychology, 67*, 148–162. https://doi.org/10.1016/j.jsp.2017.10.003

Lee, S. J. (2012). The effects of the teacher–student relationship and academic press on student engagement and academic performance. *International Journal of Educational Research*, *53*, 330–340. https://doi.org/10.1016/j.ijer.2012.04.006

Quaglia, R. J., & Corso, M. J. (2014). Student voice. Pump it up. *Principal Leadership*, *1*, 28.

Tsai, S.-F., & Cheney, D. (2012). The impact of the adult–child relationship on school adjustment for children at risk of serious behavior problems. *Journal of Emotional and Behavioral Disorders*, *20*(2), 105–114. https://doi.org/10.1177/1063426611418974

Vollet, J., Kindermann, T., & Skinner, E. (2017). In peer matters, teachers matter: Peer group influences on students' engagement depend on teacher involvement. *Journal of Educational Psychology*, *109*, 635–652. https://doi.org/10.1037/edu0000172

4

Parent/Caregiver Engagement

Remote learning has increased parent collaboration. Parents seem more invested and eager to participate in their child's programming. Remote therapy has created a perfect opportunity for education and collaboration. Parents can witness their children's skills and can carry them over more effectively at home.

– Aimee Johnson, Occupational Therapist

Throughout my investigation, one reoccurring theme was the emphasis and importance of parent engagement and involvement while students are learning remotely. Parental involvement is essential for the success of the child, especially for students with learning challenges. Parents have always been contributing members of the IEP team, and with remote learning, their involvement is vital. Recognizing most parents' competing priorities, which prevent them from always being available to assist their children during the day, is essential as an IEP team works together and figure out solutions to aid the child's success.

With the changing landscape of education and the implementation of remote learning, a great deal of pressure is added to parents working at home with children with learning challenges. For one, the typical parent does not have a teaching certificate or licensure, not to mention the tools needed to teach children with diagnosed disabilities or special education supports. Most parents are employed and have multiple children; consequently, the task is daunting and extremely challenging. As we move forward, there is a lot to learn on all fronts, especially as we figure out the specifics and logistics of remote learning for students with disabilities and learning challenges. In the meantime, it is beneficial to figure out practical and meaningful ways that parents and educators make time to work together despite all the roadblocks. Parent engagement and frequent, ongoing communication are essential for children's success with learning challenges in the remote environment.

Regardless of a family's socioeconomic status, ethnicity, or background, children with parents involved and invested in their education tend to be more successful at school. Children with engaged parents tend to have higher grades, better test scores, attend school habitually, are social, display appropriate behavior, and adjust well to school (Henderson & Mapp, 2002). The importance of parent engagement and involvement does not only apply within the walls of the school. It can translate into a remote classroom. Educators express that many successful children adapting to remote instruction have a robust support system and engaged parents.

Parents and educators must navigate the ongoing development and implementation of the IEP in partnership with everyone involved in educational decision making. Remote learning will not change parents' and educators' need to serve as a united team focusing on a child's best interest. Establishing a consistent, positive, and active relationship between the IEP team and parents is beneficial for everyone involved. The parent–educator partnership is paramount to the student's success regardless of whether they are working remotely or in-person.

When creating those partnerships, it is essential to keep in mind the diversity, differences, and families' specific needs.

The Massachusetts Department of Elementary and Secondary Education (2020) developed a road map, called *Strengthening Partnerships: A Framework for Prenatal through Young Adulthood Family Engagement in Massachusetts*, to help school and community organizations build relationships with families during remote learning and schools reopening process. Although developed in Massachusetts, the guide can be applied in communities across the country. The five guiding principles provide a foundation in creating, within systems and organizations, a culture that values and thrives on family engagement. The five principles to remember are:

1. Each family is unique and represents diverse and various family structures.
2. Acknowledging and accepting the need to engage all families is essential for engaging diverse families and recognizing strengths from their varied backgrounds.
3. Building a respectful, trusting, and reciprocal relationship is a shared responsibility of families, practitioners, organizations, and systems.
4. Families are their child's first and best advocate.
5. Family engagement must be equitable.

Additionally, the Flamboyan Foundation of Washington, D.C. (2020) has developed strategies to build relationships and partnerships with families. Those strategies suggest that schools and educators be authentic, child-centered, learn and focus on what is important to the family, offer frequent and consistent communication, and reach out to all families. See Figure 4.1 next.

Considering the guiding principles and relationship-building strategies, educators should prioritize home school partnerships while respecting families' diverse structure and needs. Keeping the partnership focused on the child is essential.

Remote learning is changing the educational landscape, but one aspect that should not change is the parents' critical role on the IEP team. Decision making and collaboration are vital as schools and parents work together to figure out all their students' individualized remote needs. Parents and educators should work as a coordinated and supportive team to form a home-school partnership built around the child's success.

The Research

Throughout my investigation, research findings reinforced the critical role that parental involvement plays in successful remote

Guiding Principles for Beginning of the Year Relationship Building

Regardless of the strategy you choose, these principles should guide your approach to building relationships with your student's families.

Be authentic.
Family engagement is people work— sharing yourself authentically with families will help quickly build trust and rapport. Creating a strong sense of shared humanity can help us feel connected.

Center on the student.
Ask about hopes, dreams, and expectations. This is an incredible opportunity for the teacher, student, and family to align on what's most important to each of them in supporting the student's academic success.

Focus on what is important to the family.
These conversations should emphasize building connections. Focus on the relationship while following the family's lead. Some families might want to share and get to know your background; others might want academic information. Many will want both!

Consistency is key.
Relationships take time. These strategies will start the process of building relationships. Still, it is frequent and consistent communication that allows relationships to grow and sustain, especially if you do not have the opportunity to connect frequently with families in-person.

All families receive outreach.
Every family deserves to have a trusting relationship with their child's teacher. Families should see that relationship building is for everyone!

This resource may be reproduced for educational, noncommercial uses only (with this copyright line): Copyright © 2020 Flamboyan Foundation; www.FlamboyanFoundation.org. All rights reserved.

FIGURE 4.1 Guiding Principles for Beginning of the Year Relationship Building From Flamboyan Foundation

Source: Flamboyan Foundation (2020).

learning. Survey results concluded that educators felt that most children who successfully adapted to remote instruction had a robust support system *and* engaged parents. Unfortunately, the survey results indicated that only 50 percent of educators felt that parental engagement was adequate, creating a significant improvement opportunity.

Strategies for Parent/Caregiver Engagement

The secret to successful parent engagement in the remote setting is to find options that work for everyone involved. Collaboration should happen almost effortlessly, given the number of challenges and expectations parents face.

Collectively, the following strategies were shared within the survey results by participating educators. Pick a few methods to try, and hopefully, it will increase parent engagement and a home school partnership.

The following are strategies suggested by educators to improve parent engagement and reinforce relationship building between the educator and the parents:

Initial Remote IEP Check-In

In addition to the annual IEP meeting, scheduling an initial remote appointment with the parents to go over the IEP is essential. It should occur at the beginning of the school year with less formal weekly check-ins with the case manager or special education teacher.

If possible, the initial remote meeting should include the special education teacher, general education teacher, and all active service providers, which could consist of the occupational therapist, physical therapist, speech and language pathologist, behavioral specialist, and assistive technology specialist. It would be beneficial if the entire IEP team members could be present at the first meeting to go over the goals of remote learning, schedules of services, and establish an ongoing communication system between each other and the parents. The meeting should also discuss daily schedules and expectations for home and school.

Parents and educators must participate in an open dialogue to explore successful accommodations for a student's IEP. Evaluation of the current IEP plan is useful to ensure that parents and educators can successfully implement it. Specifically, educators should teach parents how to implement essential parts of the IEP to help the home environment, such as Present Levels of Educational Performance A (PLEP A). PLEP A summarizes accommodations that are useful in the classroom. Suitable accommodations could include frequent breaks, verbal or visual cues, a checklist of materials, extended time on assessments, flexible seating, sensory tools, fidget to focus, reduced distractions, motor breaks, assignments broken down into smaller chunks, and noise-canceling headphones (etc.). Having such mechanisms available from parents to replicate at home can help day-to-day remote assignments by reducing sensory overload, distractions, and frustrations. Educators mention the many benefits of working with parents to replicate some of these accommodations at home.

All meetings between educators and parents should be tracked and logged (see the example in Appendix 4.1) to document communication, progress, challenges, and successes. The log can be used at the student's annual IEP meeting as a tool and referred to as additionally collected evidence to create yearly goals or make changes to appropriate accommodations.

Reach Out to Share a Positive

Reach out to parents frequently with feedback and share good news specific to their child. Maybe they helped someone who was struggling, volunteered to read aloud, or did very well on the year's first assessment. By starting with a positive note, they will feel like you appreciate their child, care about their successes, and parents will most likely be more attentive if you eventually need to contact them with some not-so-great news. Immediate communication opens the doors for ongoing communication throughout the year.

Weekly Check-Ins

Once a shared understanding among the IEP team is recognized, a schedule of services is implemented, and replications of accommodations are established. A weekly check-in has been reported as useful in modifying the accommodations and other challenges of the week.

A scheduled weekly check-in meeting guarantees that everyone is on the same page. If a student is falling behind, it is imperative to catch it immediately. With a scheduled weekly meeting, educators will know to be vigilant in keeping track of their students' progress. Parents alleviate the risk of any end-of-semester assignment shock or surprise failures (Welby, 2020).

Additionally, parents and educators benefit from open communication regarding the trial and error of accommodations to establish a coherent plan to move forward. These weekly check-ins can be a phone call, a virtual meeting, a shared Google Document, or a weekly email, depending on the parents' and educators' availability. On the same document (Appendix 4.1), note the communication and progress of the student.

Depending on the student's age and cognitive ability, the student could be involved in the weekly check-in if deemed appropriate.

Mail Handwritten Thank-You Notes

Service providers, therapists, and teachers all mentioned the power of handwritten, mailed, thank-you notes. Therapists have sent parents thank-you notes after they participated in services and noticed it increased their interest and excitement during future services. Teachers also mentioned that they have handwritten and mailed thank-you notes to parents after a challenging conversation or after a meeting. That small extra communication has strengthened the relationship and partnership.

Coffee Hour

Donate an hour or two a week for a drop-in coffee hour for parents to check in. Educators mention that they have a virtual meeting open, such as Zoom or Google Meets, while they work or grade, and parents have the option to pop in and ask a question or address a concern if they choose to. The extra meeting time opens up communication lines if parents feel a meeting or check-in is needed.

Parent Collaboration Events

Educators are creating voluntary parent collaboration events they facilitate. For example, a special educator reached out to all the parents on their caseload and invited them to a coffee talk one evening. During that time, she led the discussion focused on the remote learning classroom's successes and challenges through the parents' eyes. She collected anecdotal data to improve her practices by listening and giving her parents a voice. Parents continued to meet on their own and formed a support group.

Parent Workshops
School districts are offering virtual parent workshops on an Introduction to Special Education to help parents understand the impact disabilities have on learning. Additionally, various school districts are sharing tools to implement positive behavior management strategies, tips for accommodation implementations, and overviews on augmented communication devices in the home setting. Teachers, service providers, and administrators provide these workshops and note the success in improving parent engagement. Some record the meetings and workshops and can send to parents at later dates if a struggle emerges.

Weekly Goal Setting
Choose an IEP objective each week to focus on with your students and share with parents so they can reinforce it at home. Having too many goals, assignments, and expectations has led to failure and reduced student motivation. Ensure the learning goal is aligned to the annual IEP goals, and, most importantly, the learning goal is reinforced throughout the week by both parents and educators. By verbalizing and displaying this learning goal, educators will help the student recognize the *why* behind the lesson, understand the expectations, work toward a specific accomplishment, and take ownership of achieving the goal. Keep the goal and expectation clear and concise.

Create a General Communication Hub
Maintain a centralized location for generalized communication to your students' parents – a communication hub where you can keep parents updated and informed throughout the year. If the school has an existing learning platform such as Blackboard or Canvas,

use that and teach parents how to access and utilize your class site to stay informed. If the school did not invest in a venue, there are online tools available such as Google Classroom, Padlet, or ClassDojo.

This general communication hub includes any school updates, general emails sent, instructions for completing and submitting work, teacher contact information and office hours, reminders regarding half days, or school closure dates.

The communication hub could also include prerecorded videos and tutorials. Some suggested tutorials could include an overview of the components of an IEP and where to find annual goals and accommodations, do it yourself (DIY) sensory path instructions, DIY accommodations, DIY sensory tools, and suggested flexible seating options.

Additionally, the communication hub could include your recorded lessons that parents can reference to reinforce at home. Service providers could post videos of generalized service reinforcers and videos on essential at-home functions such as supporting correct pencil grip at home or physical therapy tips that will increase accessibility in the school building upon return.

Educators can record and create videos using web conferencing applications such as Zoom, Google Meet, and Adobe Connect. They can use video recording tools such as Loom or Screencast-O-Matic, or use a phone or other webcam recording computer or device and post on the designated communication hub.

Weekly Newsletter and Updates

Educators note the importance of keeping families in the loop by sending out weekly newsletters and updates on what is going on in the remote classroom. Some educators send digital newsletters with contact information of all teachers, administrators, and links to assignments.

Post Assignments or Slides Sunday Night

Sharing slides, assignments, service provider goals, and study guides before the school week were mentioned frequently. Parents appreciate the advance notice for learning goals and have an opportunity to forecast the week and prepare.

Service Delivery Participation

Occupational therapists (OTs), physical therapists (PTs), and speech and language pathologists (SLPs) report that the most significant benefit to providing services remotely is the increased parent involvement, active participation, and interest. Many service providers are re-creating services to involve fun activities that parents can participate in with their children while the therapist is watching virtually and making suggestions. The benefits have increased the reinforcement of IEP goals and parent engagement at home.

Some case managers and special education teachers try to schedule therapists simultaneously and work on a coordinated lesson, typically working together with the student for 45 minutes, then meeting with the parents. The parents have access to all the therapists to meet and ask questions, and the children are not overscheduled with therapy times during the remote day. This may need approval from the district administration and may not work for all school districts. Combined service delivery was mentioned multiple times within the survey. Parents seem to prefer the all at the one-time method and appreciate the scheduled time to talk to the therapists without overwhelming their child with an overload of therapies throughout each day.

Recorded Lessons

Educators find it helpful to share prerecorded lessons and share with families. They note it is a successful way to increase parent engagement. Some educators also record the synchronous classes and share the videos with parents to reinforce the content learned that day. Other educators record lessons when they know that the topic is challenging and share it before the lesson with students. The child can reference the videos for additional needed support, and the parents can watch the videos to understand the content taught (Welby, 2020).

Parent engagement is vital for goal setting and accomplishments of all students working in the remote learning environment, even more so for students with documented disabilities with IEPs.

It is beneficial for parents and educators to determine what is best for the child right now. Parent engagement and ongoing communication are essential for children diagnosed with disabilities in the remote learning environment.

Success Story

Jennifer, a preK–12 teacher of the deaf from Iowa, creates a communication journal shared Google document with parents to track IEP goals.

Parents and educators could write in the Google document when they need to share something about the child. Everyone with access can view the document in real-time, on their own, and see immediate updates, challenges, and successes without having to schedule additional meetings to discuss. Together they can keep communication open and record how the child is doing while keeping track and documenting IEP goal progress. Such documentation does not take up too much time and can be referenced during IEP meetings and viewed weekly. Plus all members can view, read, and add in their own time.

An additional idea to this suggestion could be to invite all service providers (OT, PT, SLP) to document the progress of IEP goals and have parents also add home progress to OT, PT, and speech IEP goals.

Quick Tips From Educators

Alisha, a general education high school teacher from Arizona, recommends not to send out too many emails to parents. You do not want to bombard them, and you want to ensure they read what you send. The key is to send them an email when you notice a pattern or the student is missing a significant number of assignments. This way, when you reach out to them, parents recognize the communication as crucial.

Monique, a K–2 special education teacher from Rhode Island, recommends being aware of family schedules. As difficult as it is, you may need to work around their needs and be flexible if you want engagement.

Lucy, a K–5 special education teacher in Massachusetts, recommends calling the parent at the start of the school year to find out previous challenges of remote learning, go over the child's daily schedule, and explain schoolwork expectations.

Jennifer, a middle school special education teacher from Utah, recommends emailing both parents immediately if their child did not log into live instruction. Sometimes students get sidetracked or are asleep. By informing their parents immediately, she has strengthened her relationship with her parents because they appreciate the communication. It has also immensely helped with improved attendance.

Leigh, an intensive needs high school special educator from Colorado, sends weekly assignments to parents. These optional extension activities give the parents an idea and insight into what their child is working on. These assignments have led to a discussion on the topic between the parent and the child. Knowing what their child is doing can increase engagement.

Jonah, a general education high school teacher from Idaho, has found it helpful to invite parents of children with intensive needs to attend individual or live classroom meetings.

 Highlighted Resource

Commonsense.org has an abundance of already created downloadable documents that are free of charge and can be personalized to meet the needs of your remote classroom. There are templates to create your classroom Q&A sheet, a customizable progress tracker for parents, a weekly learning plan template, and digital learning routine expectations that can help communicate with families. Additionally, there are many additional downloadable templates to help create opportunities for communication and parent engagement. Here is the resource link: www.commonsense.org/education/articles/free-distance-learning-templates-for-back-to-school

Remember

- ✓ Parent and educator partnerships are critical for the success of the student.
- ✓ Communicate weekly through phone conversations, email, or virtual meeting and document conversations by tracking students' successes and challenges.
- ✓ Set a weekly student achievement goal. Parents and teachers reinforce the same goal.
- ✓ Keep all communication, contact information, and essential information in one place and make sure parents know how to access the information.
- ✓ Include parents in service delivery such as occupational therapy (OT), speech and language therapy, and physical therapy (PT) as much as possible.
- ✓ Little things such as a mailed thank-you note or a check-in phone call show parents that educators value and are invested in their relationship.

4.1

Appendix: Sample Remote Home/School Communication Document

ABC School District

Remote Documentation – Weekly Parent Communication

Student Name	
Date of Birth	
Parent/Guardian	
Parent/Guardian Contact Information	
Case Manager/Teacher	
Case Manager/Teacher Contact Information	
IEP Goals	
Service Delivery	
Remote Accommodations	
Pre-determined Meeting Dates and Times	

Date of Communication	Virtual Communication	Weekly Home/School Goal	Weekly Remote Successes and Challenges	IEP Progress Monitoring	Other Notes or Actions Needed
	Email Phone Text Virtual Platform				
	Email Phone Text Virtual Platform				
	Email Phone Text Virtual Platform				
	Email Phone Text Virtual Platform				
	Email Phone Text Virtual Platform				
	Email Phone Text Virtual Platform				
	Email Phone Text Virtual Platform				
	Email Phone Text Virtual Platform				

References

Flamboyan Foundation. (2020). *Beginning of the year relationship building toolkit*. Retrieved from https://flamboyanfoundation.org/resource/beginning-of-the-year-relationship-building-toolkit/

Henderson, A., & Mapp, K. (2002). *A new wave of evidence: The impact of school, parent and community connections on student achievement* (p. 7). Austin, TX: Southwest Educational Development Laboratory. Retrieved from https://sedl.org/connections/resources/evidence.pdf

The Massachusetts Department of Elementary and Secondary Education. (2020). *Strengthening partnerships: A framework for prenatal through young adulthood family engagement in Massachusetts*. Retrieved from www.doe.mass.edu/sfs/family-engagement-framework.pdf

Welby, K. (2020). *Remote school round 2: How to improve distance learning for students with ADHD*. Retrieved from www.additudemag.com/distance-learning-adhd-iep-504-plan/

5

The Remote IEP Meeting

So many positives have come about from the virtual IEP meeting. Most parents are more engaged and involved in the process and the feedback is that they have more flexibility to attend meetings as they do not need to take time out of work to participate. Parents can join at lunch or take a break throughout the day without having to drive anywhere. As a whole, the IEP teams have given feedback that the meetings are more efficient, student-focused, and have targeted outcomes. Also, documents are signed digitally rather than through snail mail so children can start to receive services immediately – there is no wait time! The virtual IEP meeting may be one of the options post-COVID that will be the preferred meeting type of the future. It is working out very well for the majority of parents and staff involved.
– Massachusetts Special Education Administrator

Remote IEP meetings were used more frequently as a temporary solution to the inability to conduct in-person meetings due to schools' closure in 2020. The Individuals with Disabilities Education Act (IDEA) allows the IEP team to use alternative means of meeting participation. Opportunely, the forced change of alternative delivery methods, such as remote meetings, will most likely turn into the preferred choice for team meetings.

The convenience of remote meetings has been a well-received turning point for most parents and school districts. Parents can attend more easily during the day without a need to leave work or find childcare. Although IEP team members no longer see each other in the hall to schedule meetings or pop into classes, the scheduling process is far easier to coordinate a virtual meeting among all the team members without any need to consider travel time. Furthermore, many participants have found the remote IEP more efficient and effective than the traditional approach keeping everyone on track and student-focused.

The forced change of the remote IEP meeting seems to have proven beneficial. It will most likely stick around for the long haul – especially if school districts adhere to the federal guidelines, follow protocol for IEPs under the IDEA, gather IEP-related documentation, guarantee that all team members have access to technology, and ensure that professional dispositions and behavior are of high quality.

Individuals with Disabilities Education Act (IDEA)

As mentioned in Chapter 2, IDEA mandates that all children, regardless of disabilities and learning challenges, are entitled to a free and appropriate public education. Current law does not allow for any special circumstances. Even if schools are closed, creating substantial challenges to the special education community, the federal government would not recommend any waivers to affect IDEA. All students are expected to receive all academics assurances outlined in a child's IEP to guarantee that academic commitments are met. In doing so, regardless of location, if all team members and parents agree, IEP meetings will continue even if carried out in a remote environment.

Types of Remote IEP Meetings

Each type of IEP meeting should be focused on understanding the student. Every IEP should include sufficient detail to allow complete understanding by someone unfamiliar with the student. The different meetings – initial, annual, and triennial/reevaluation – can be carried out remotely. Next are descriptions of the IEP meeting that can be carried out remotely.

Initial: The initial IEP meeting can be held remotely. The initial meeting is held for students who currently do not receive special education services but were evaluated for possible disabilities that could qualify for services. At this initial meeting, if the student qualifies for special education services, the team will discuss the best plan for the student, services provided, and, together, develop goals, accommodations, and modifications.

Annual: After the initial IEP meeting, every year that follows, an annual meeting should occur to discuss the progress and achievement of goals and objectives. This meeting will address the present performance levels, successes, challenges, and other relevant information and progress. According to IDEA (2004), the IEP meeting must happen periodically, but not less often than annually, to decide whether the child's annual goals are being achieved. The annual IEP meeting can be held remotely.

Triennial/Reevaluation: The timeline for reevaluation meetings is three years. During the reevaluation meeting, the IEP team decides if there is a need to terminate the terms of the IEP if the child is no longer eligible or if services are no longer necessary for a child to make progress. The appropriate and qualified team member will often conduct formal academic and other needed formalized testing, and the results are discussed at the reevaluation meeting. The reevaluation meeting can be held remotely.

Amendments: Amendment meetings are sometimes necessary to change or adjust the initial terms of the IEP. Frequently, and depending on which state you live in, the sudden switch to remote learning required amendments and adjustments to the current IEPs to increase learning accessibility to be conducive to the remote learning environment.

Initial, annual, triennial/reevaluation, and amendment meetings can be successful in the remote environment. Attendance policies, proper distribution of documentation, and preparation are critical in the meeting delivery's success.

Attendance at the Remote IEP Meeting

During the remote IEP meeting, the team of stakeholders discusses the specifics of the student's report and progress. The team members can vary, but typically include parents/guardians, a general education teacher, a special education teacher, a school district representative, an expert to interpret evaluation results, the student, an assortment of learning specialists, and service providers such as occupational therapists, physical therapists, and counselors. The transition to the remote IEP meeting does not mean the attendance expectations change; it simply changes the location of those attending. The following IEP team members' role and participation are described next:

Parent/guardian: Parents are part of the IEP team and can provide information regarding their child's strengths, struggles, and goals. They can also provide information on their child's remote learning experience from the parent and home perspective.

General education teachers: General education teachers can report how they are doing in the remote general education environment.

Special education teachers: The special education teachers offer input on what they need to thrive in the remote general education environment. Suggestions may include how to modify remote instruction or offer remote accommodations for the student's needs.

A school district representative: The IEP must include someone, such as an administrator, who can approve school resources. This person must be qualified to supervise remote special education services.

An expert who can interpret evaluation results: The expert could be an existing team member such as the special education administrator, school psychologist, or the special education teacher. The individual must interpret evaluation results and explain how parents can understand by minimizing jargon and acronyms.

The child: The student can be included on the team. A student can self-advocate for resources he or she may need to be successful in the remote environment and develop the transition plan.

A translator: The school district must provide an interpreter in the parents' primary language if needed.

Additional Personnel: Additional individuals with the knowledge or distinct expertise regarding the child, including related services personnel as appropriate and at the discretion of the parent or the agency.

Depending on the specific type of IEP meeting, all persons described previously, including invited participants such as service delivery providers, outside agencies, special education advocates, and others, are still expected to attend remote IEP meetings to discuss the student's reports and progress. If anyone cannot participate, advance notification is expected and possible delay or rescheduling of the meeting.

Documents

IEPs are legal documents between a student, family, and the district. The same documentation required for in-person meetings is required during the virtual meeting. Such documents include prior written notice, meeting notice, a final notice of recommendation, attendance sheets, special education guidelines, parental rights, evaluation reports, progress reports, the IEP, copies of sample work, and other documents. Make sure to transfer all documents to a digital format to allow digital signatures to ease the transition. Some suggested software for digital forms and signatures are DocuSign and Smallpdf.

The Research

This section contains strategies discussed with district leadership, building administrators, service delivery professionals, special education teachers, and general education teachers during interviews and gathered from survey results. The information provided was collected through various special education documents such as participation guides, IEP remote agenda documents, remote tutorials, remote meeting norms, etiquette guides, and faculty Q&A documents collected from school districts across the US. The records were analyzed and combined, and the most relevant information is shared later. Most school systems broke down norms and requirements into three distinct areas – before the IEP meeting, during the IEP meeting, and after the IEP meeting.

Additionally, some of the information in this section, specifically Figure 5.1, highlight the IEP norms, roles, and agendas developed through outside experts. The group received an Office of Special Education Program (OSEP) grant. The figure was created collaboratively with the PROGRESS Centers; the Center for Appropriate Dispute Resolution in Special Education; Center for

Parent Information and Resources; Family Network on Disabilities; National Center for Systemic Improvement; and Wisconsin Family Assistance Center for Education, Training, and Support. Many of their findings were parallel to the findings I had throughout the investigation into the IEP meeting. Their collaborative research is noteworthy and strengthens many findings from the interviews and collected documents. The link to all of their resources is highlighted in the resource section of this chapter.

The next part of this chapter will provide tips for educators to facilitate successful remote IEP meetings. The information shared was created by analyzing the collected ideas and themes of the participant survey and interviews and in the calibration of collected district documents.

District-Level Suggestions

For consistency, the following protocols, such as district professional development, email confidentiality, establishing norms, meeting roles, and a library of "how-to videos" would help transition from in-person IEP meetings to remote. Most of the following protocols could be established and communicated from administration to all the educators involved in remote IEP meetings.

Professional Development: District professional development is a critical first step in developing consistency of IEP remote meeting norms, expectations, and requirements for all schools within a district. Once the district has established standard expectations and needs, a checklist can be developed based on the specific requirements for proper implementation (Appendix 5.1 is a sample checklist created by combining all important collected information). Consistency between all the schools within the district is essential. This is especially important because some service providers travel between schools with multiple children at several schools on their caseload.

Email Confidentiality: Without in-person contact, there will be an increase in email communications between the IEP team, which increases confidentiality expectations. Gmail and Outlook both have confidentiality modes that can be enabled to offer protection against unauthorized sharing and forwarding. Enabling confidentiality features are essential.

Establishing Norms: Developing and communicating expected norms for IEP meetings is essential because of the meeting structure's efficacy. Each district may have different considerations, so understanding the district demographics and needs is vital in establishing norms. Each district can establish criteria based on needs. The following are some remote IEP meeting norms suggested by educators:

- Stay present and engaged.
- Mute if you are not speaking.
- Encourage district personal cameras to be on throughout the meeting.
- Monitor your talk time.
- Build trust and safety.
- Provide an agenda and stick to it.
- The facilitator must redirect to the agenda if the discussion begins to go off track.
- Monitor time.
- Stay student-centered.
- Be mindful of your surroundings.
- Be mindful of what tabs are open or what is on your screen if screen sharing.
- All IEP requirements still apply to remote meetings.
- Dress professionally.
- End the meeting with a checkout to avoid misunderstandings. Discuss excitements, positives, challenges, and concerns, and allow time for questions.
- The facilitator reminds the group if a norm has been broken.

In addition to the educator-suggested IEP meeting norms, Figure 5.1 also recommends five meeting norms. Developing district-wide standards rather than school-based models helps administrators and service providers who support multiple schools. The specific norms can be decided based on district needs and expectations, but the bottom line should be some rules and consistency.

Consistency of Platform: Knowing that IEP team members such as occupational therapists, physical therapists, speech and language pathologists, and other service providers or outside agencies could be traveling and working at different schools within the same district, it is helpful if all schools in the same district decide on a single platform to use for consistency. Service providers have noted confusion about having to adapt to different platforms at different schools. Of course, if parents do not have access or if a telephone conference is needed, be sure to create a backup plan.

Agenda Consistency: Creating an agenda that can be replicated for each student keeps all the meetings consistent and on track. Administrators noted the benefits of creating a district-wide agenda to ensure all critical areas of the IEP are discussed. Figure 5.1 provides a sample schedule.

Roles: School personnel who are team members should have preassigned roles to ensure fluency and accountability. The specifics of the roles could be decided within the school district. For example, the following illustration suggests that remote IEP meetings have a facilitator, timekeeper, scribe, and notetaker. Specifically, Figure 5.1 is a sample virtual meeting agenda, which is produced under the US Department of Education and shows the recommended responsibilities of each role.

Create How-To Videos: Having a district-wide location for collecting "how-to videos tutorials" has been helpful. Educators suggest the dissemination of the videos when prepping and planning for IEP meetings and as a follow-up. Creating a variety of videos for educators, parents, and outside agencies have proved successful. Spending the time initially creating the videos saves time and energy with less constant and repeated instructions to team members. How-to videos could include Technology 101, How to Zoom (or use district chosen platform), clips on IEP remote meeting etiquette and expectations, digital doc sign instructions, IEP reading tips, home accommodation suggestions, DIY sensory tool recipes, and tips. When sending out documents pre- and post-IEP meetings, send out a video to follow and prepare. Most educators interviewed use YouTube, while others use Flipgrid or recorded Zoom as their preferred video library platform.

These suggestions, establishing norms, agendas, meeting roles, creating "how-to videos", deciding on a consistent video conferencing platform, and increased privacy measures could be discussed at a district-wide professional development meeting with all the stakeholders involved. Proper preparation and communication

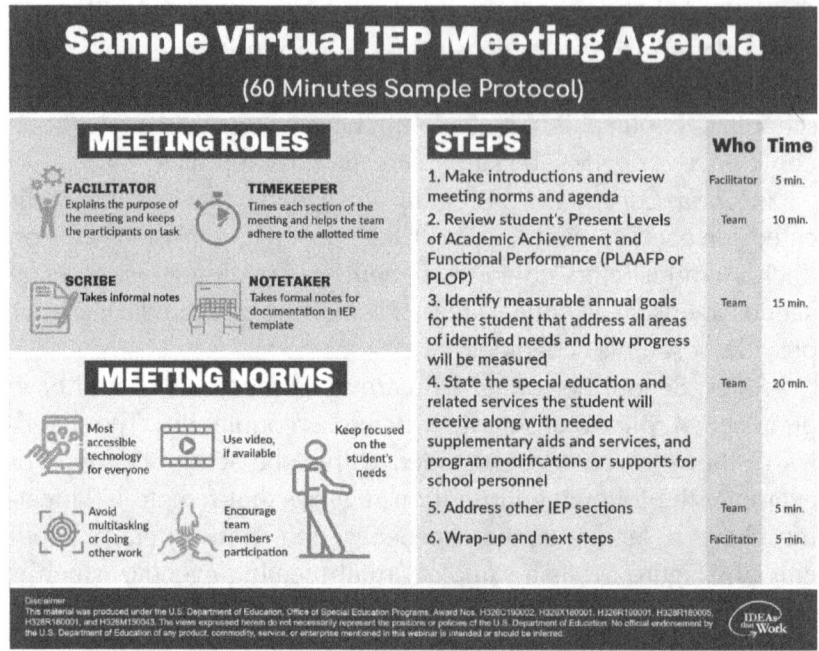

FIGURE 5.1 Sample Virtual IEP Meeting Agenda

Source: Was developed through an OSEP grant by the PROGRESS Center, The Center for Appropriate Dispute Resolution in Special Education, Center for Parent Information and Resources, Family Network on Disabilities, National Center for Systemic Improvement and Wisconsin Family Assistance Center for Education, Training, and Support. Retrieved from Tips for Facilitating Successful Virtual IEP Meetings During a Pandemic and Beyond (2020, October 6).

will ease the transition to remote IEP meetings, especially if the concept is new to educators. Consistency within a district is helpful because so many service providers, educators, and administrators attend IEP meetings at various schools within the same district.

IEP Meeting Preparation

The time and energy devoted to the preparation of the IEP meeting are significant. The time dedicated to advanced groundwork ensures the process moves smoothly. Remote IEP meetings require just as much preparation and possibly more than in-person meetings. Here are suggestions for preparing for remote IEP meetings.

Appendix 5.1 is a checklist resource to help prepare for meetings, engage in the meeting, and follow up after meetings.

Check in With teachers: Have a quick conversation with the students' teachers to determine what is working and what is not working in the remote learning environment. Collecting and documenting data and anecdotal notes will prepare you for the possible suggestions the student will need to be successful remotely. The team meeting is an excellent opportunity to discuss those suggestions and brainstorm remote accommodations.

Send Home All Documents: Before the IEP meeting, digitally prepare all documents (prior written notice, meeting notice, a final notice of recommendation, attendance sheets, special education guidelines, and parental rights, all evaluation reports, progress reports, the IEP, copies of sample work, and other documents needed for the particular type of IEP meeting) and send to parents through an email. If digital delivery is not preferred, send all forms through the mail, but leave plenty of time for distribution and transport.

Add Record Restriction Language to IEP Invite: Add language to the IEP meeting invite to discourage meeting recordings. Different school districts had various variations, and here is a highlighted example used in one Massachusetts School District:

> *The IEP Team meeting is being held remotely upon agreement of the parents/guardians. By participating in the remote IEP meeting, the participants agree not to save, record, share, or post the IEP meeting. The district will take all reasonable measures to preserve your privacy and the privacy of your child, and each of our educators will continue to maintain the privacy of your child's student record information.*

Schedule Times With Consideration of Technology: Many educators mentioned that scheduling IEP meetings too close to each other could lead to problems such as the technology learning curve among participants. Allow extra time for participants to learn the technology, address bad connections, or handle any technology mistakes and challenges that can occur.

Contact Parents/Guardian: Reach out to parents/guardians before the IEP meeting to determine their comfort level and experience with video conferencing platforms. If they need support, send them "How to Videos" from the established district video library. If they do not have access to technology, discuss the option of a phone conference. Answer any housekeeping and logistical questions prior.

You can also do a pre-conference check-in and ask about the student's progress at home. Have a quick conversation to find out some successes and challenges happening in the remote learning environment. Be sure to share with the team at the meeting, but talking prior will help prepare some solutions to be discussed the day of the meeting.

Encourage Student Participation: According to IDEA, students should attend their IEP meetings whenever appropriate. Depending on age and cognitive ability, students should be continued to be invited even when sessions are remote. This is an excellent opportunity for students to share screens and show their work to the group. They can and should be part of the discussion and solution.

Establish Roles and Assign Tasks: If your district has identified dedicated roles (facilitator, timekeeper, scribe, and notetaker) for IEP meetings, ensure those roles are assigned before the meeting to alleviate confusion. At the beginning of the meeting, remind each person of his or her role.

Create the Agenda/Access the District-Wide "Normed" Agenda: Create the agenda before the meeting and share the agenda before the meeting and during the session using the chat screen or posting it through screen share. The schedule will keep the discussion on track and focused. (Reference Appendix 5.1.)

Accommodation Needs: Reach out to the team to determine if any team member requires accommodations such as a closed caption or a translator.

Notify Parents/Guardian of Absent Team Members: As you would any IEP meeting, notify parents before the meeting if any team member will be absent.

Be Ready to Pivot: Establish a backup plan before the IEP meeting to alleviate the scramble. With remote IEP meetings, you are relying on the technology of every team member to run smoothly. Send out a telephone conferencing number as a backup plan to the video conferencing platform you planned on using.

The IEP Meeting

The IEP meetings are an opportunity to gather with the entire team and ensure students are working to meet their potential. While these meetings are a review of a legal document, they are also an opportunity for the team to create a working plan of what works best for the student. Embrace the conference as a time to gather and focus on the student's success and the student's remote learning needs. All the details that would have to be discussed during the in-person IEP meeting must be addressed in the remote IEP meeting. When engaged in an IEP meeting, remember to use parent-friendly language, minimizing educational jargon and special education acronyms. Here are tips to make the logistics of the remote meeting a success.

Camera On/Camera Off: Establish if the team plans to have their cameras on or off. If the camera is on, be aware of your surroundings and background.

Off the Record Chat: IEP meetings can be stressful, and parents may be anxious. Introduce all team members and start the session with a quick chat or check-in to ease the nerves of all attending. Another suggestion was to start with a question that will help people connect personally – having a short off the record chat before the meeting can build trust and increase participation and engagement.

Establish Meeting Norms: The facilitator should start the meeting by reviewing the meeting purpose and discussing the meeting norms, schedule, and roles of the team members.

Stick to Agenda: The IEP agenda should be the same as in-person covering all areas of the IEP. See Figure 5.1 for a sample (or refer to Appendix 5.1). If the agenda was established district-wide, make sure the schedule is followed. The facilitator should be responsible for bringing everyone back on track and redirect all to the agenda if the meeting or discussion gets off track at any point. The schedule can be posted in the meeting chat or shared screen.

Document Conversation: The scribe and notetaker should document the conversation of the meeting. At the end of the session, notetakers should review their notes to confirm everything was documented accurately, possibly even displaying the notes using a shared screen.

Professionalism: Dress and act as professional as you would with an in-person meeting. Do not multitask, be mindful of your surroundings, and find a quiet place to participate in the discussion. The IEP meeting should remain student-focused.

Share Screens: Sharing screen has been a helpful feature for the remote IEP meeting. Sharing, highlighting, and explaining student work is more straightforward. The notetaker and scribe can take notes throughout and display them at the end to make sure the meeting notes were captured correctly. Additionally, the IEP template can be filled out and displayed throughout using the meeting's conversation as a guide.

All Voices Are Heard: During the IEP meeting, everyone should be self-aware of their "talk time" and try not to dominate the conversation. Everyone has something to share, so the facilitator should guide the meeting to hear all voices. It is not recommended to mute the parent at any point in the meeting unless they mute themselves.

Confirm Understanding: End the meeting by sharing the documented notes taken throughout and allow time to comment and ask questions. Additionally, leave time for people to share concerns.

The logistical suggestions listed previously are to help the flow and process of the remote IEP meeting. The meeting's content should not differ from the in-person meeting, and all laws outlined by IDEA still need to be followed and regulated. After the IEP, note the challenges and successes to incorporate in the future.

After the IEP Meeting

Following the IEP meeting, communicate due dates for action items from the agenda, and ensure all the required documents are signed and collected as they would for in-person meetings. Using a doc sign app may be the easiest method of remote signature collections. If remote IEP meetings are relatively new to the attendees, consider soliciting feedback from all IEP team members on improving the effectiveness of future remote sessions. This could be done using a quick survey tool such as Google Forms or SurveyMonkey to collect data on experience.

Remote IEP meetings can be as effective as in-person meetings, or even more so, by strong planning and preparation. Having roles, norms, access to technology, and an outlined plan can ensure successful implementation of the remote IEP meeting (see Appendix 5.1). Additionally, following the federal guideline under the IDEA, gathering IEP-related documentation, assuring that all team members have access to technology, and guaranteeing that professional dispositions, demeanor, and behavior are of high quality can lead to a successful future of remote IEP meetings.

Success Story

Gina, a district special education administrator from Massachusetts, has had great success with family engagement, team participation, and focus. She suggests that meeting virtually has knocked down barriers in her school district. Parents' attendance and participation are way up. Parents are no longer expected to come into school for the meetings, therefore alleviating childcare and transportation obstacles. She has watched educators and parents participate more because there seems to be less stage fright for parents when everyone is on an even playing field. Additionally, she notices her staff more confident and comfortable in virtual meetings.

Quick Tips From Educators

Mike, a K–8 building administrator in Maine, suggests following an agenda flow chart with a blank section for meeting notes during IEP meetings. He recommends taking meeting notes right on the flow cart and sharing your screen as you document the meeting. The flow chart acts as an agenda, but it also keeps the meeting student-focused, and the accuracy of the meeting minutes is displayed in real-time.

Kellie, a K–8 special education administrator in Massachusetts, suggests providing the parents with a description of how the IEP meetings will be carried out in the remote environment and listing their participation options, whether it be phone or video. She also suggests offering parents a test run before their first time attending a remote IEP meeting to alleviate any challenges on the day of the meeting.

Melissa, a special education teacher in South Carolina, recommends using the Remind app to send parents confirmations regarding meeting times and dates.

Brenda, an occupational therapist from Michigan, recommends that districts establish a uniform meeting platform, schedule, and district-wide meeting norms. When traveling to multiple schools within a district, it is simpler if all schools were consistent in meeting the service providers and outside agencies' meeting requirements.

 ## Highlighted Resource

The PROGRESS Center provides valuable information, resources, downloadable documents, informative webinars, professional development, and other tools at no cost for school districts that help facilitate a successful virtual IEP meeting. The resources can be found at this address: https://promotingprogress.org/resources/tips-facilitating-successful-virtual-iep-meetings-during-pandemic-and-beyond

The PROGRESS Center collaborated with the Center for Appropriate Dispute Resolution in Special Education; Center for Parent Information and Resources; Family Network on Disabilities; National Center for Systemic Improvement; and Wisconsin Family Assistance Center for Education, Training, and Support to create all the resources previously mentioned and located on the website.

 ## Remember

✓ The IEP meeting location may have changed, but schools must not waive the laws that schools must adhere to.

- ✓ Embrace the remote IEP meeting as a time to gather and focus on the success of the student and an opportunity to discuss the remote learning needs of the student.
- ✓ All documents required when meetings were held on the ground and in person are required during the virtual meeting.
- ✓ Make sure to transfer all documents to a digital format that will allow digital signatures.
- ✓ Remote IEP meetings can be as effective as in-person meetings by proper logistical and personnel preparation.
- ✓ Checklists and meeting outlines are helpful for notetaking and documentation (see Appendix 5.1).
- ✓ Roles, norms, access to technology, and an outlined agenda can ensure successful implementation of the remote IEP meeting.
- ✓ When engaged in a virtual IEP meeting, remember to use parent-friendly language, minimizing educational jargon and special education acronyms.
- ✓ Remote IEP meeting could be the preferred method of the future if school districts can adhere to the federal guidelines, follow protocol for IEPs under the IDEA, gather IEP-related documentation, guarantee that all team members have access to technology, and ensure that professional dispositions and behavior are of high quality.

5.1

Appendix: Sample One Page Reference – Remote IEP Meeting Checklist

ABC School District

Remote IEP Meeting Checklist

✓	Preparation for the Remote IEP Meeting
	Update privacy settings on emails.
	Check in with teachers and service providers regarding student and upcoming IEP meeting.
	Schedule meeting day and time.
	Send parent/guardians all required IEP documents.
	Add record restriction to IEP meeting invite.
	Communicate virtual platform use and email all team members links to join the meeting.
	Contact parents/guardians to ask about virtual comfort level and access to technology.
	Email parents/guardians video tutorials if needed.
	Encourage student participation if appropriate.
	Establish IEP meeting roles, norms, and assign tasks (Internal).
	Create the agenda or access the district agenda.
	Organize meeting accommodations or translator if needed.

	Notify parents/guardians of an absent team member.
	Plan for technology issues and establish a Plan B such as a phone conference.
✓	**The Remote IEP Meeting Agenda – Initial and Reevaluations (Sample)**
	Introductions: names and roles.
	Establish virtual norms and share roles and tasks.
	Confirm that the IEP meeting is not recorded and ask no one record meeting without prior authorization.
	Review agenda – post in chat or screen share.
	State purpose of the meeting, including the reason for referral.
	Ask parents/guardians about students' progress, successes, challenges, and adjustment to remote learning.
	Classroom teacher reports out on progress.
	Review testing – begin with the school psychologist and followed by academic testing and then service providers (OT, PT, S&LP).
	Parent/guardian – any questions regarding testing.
	Determine special education eligibility using an IDEA eligibility flowchart – if eligible, continue. If not eligible to receive special education services, summarize the meeting, and ask parents to sign a digital copy of the meeting summary. Give parents a digital copy of the summary.
	If the student is eligible, discuss the IEP teams' vision (including transition planning if appropriate).
	Discuss student strengths.
	Discuss IEP accommodations – presentation, setting, response, timing in remote classroom, other settings, and assessments.
	Discuss IEP goal focus area(s).
	Discuss service delivery.
	Discuss eligibility for extended year services.
	Discuss eligibility for transportation (if hybrid or blended model).
	If applicable, discuss counseling needs, home services, AAC services, outside services.
	Discuss remote classroom placement and delivery – understand placement if in-person classes resume such as full inclusion, partial inclusion, or a substantially separate program.
	Summarize meeting.
	Parents/guardians sign meeting summary and member excusal if needed.
	Give parent/guardian a digital copy of the meeting summary and tell them the next steps.

(Continued)

(Continued)

✓	After the IEP Meeting
	Develop the IEP using testing results and notes from the IEP meeting and send parents IEP for signature.
	Email or mail all appropriate documents to parents/guardians for signature.
	Survey the IEP team to collect data on effectiveness of the remote IEP and use data to improve future virtual IEP meetings.
	Parents sign the proposed IEP and student will start or continue to receive IEP services.

References

Individuals with Disabilities Education Act. (2004). https://sites.ed.gov/idea/
Tips for Facilitating Successful Virtual IEP Meetings During a Pandemic and Beyond. (2020, October 6). Retrieved from https://promotingprogress.org/resources/tips-facilitating-successful-virtual-iep-meetings-during-pandemic-and-beyond

6

Remote Accommodations and Assistive Technology

> *During remote learning, I had many students using augmentative communication (AAC) devices or AAC apps on their iPads. Having the parents present is very valuable for following through and applying the devices in the remote learning environment. I'm a firm believer that language and communication doesn't happen in a vacuum of a few short sessions in a week. By helping parents understand what a speech and language pathologist does, they can better reinforce the technology throughout their children's learning at home. Such accommodations can be a huge benefit of the remote learning environment.*
> *– Christine Derse, Speech and Language Pathologist*

Accommodations and assistive technology are essential in the remote learning environment for students with IEPs. Still, the question is, how do the outlined accommodations listed on the IEP translate to the remote home learning space?

Accommodations are used to describe an alteration of the presentation, setting, response, or schedule/time in the curriculum format that allows students with disabilities to access the content taught in school without changing the standards or expectations (Smith, Tyler, & Skow, 2018). Accommodations do not alter what is taught or the expectations of learning curriculum frameworks. Many accommodations can be replicated at home. Educators can work with parents and caregivers to ensure that the tools are available to assist, such as educational technology, virtual apps, or various assistive technology options.

Assistive technology is a type of accommodation, and in the remote learning environment, many of the typically used accommodations can also be classified as assistive technology. With the potential for enhancing learning outcomes for students with disabilities and learning challenges, the United States' federal government, in the reauthorization of the Individuals with Disabilities Education Act (IDEA, 2004), mandates that assistive technology (AT) devices be considered for every child with a disability.

Under IDEA (2004), assistive technology is defined as "any item, piece of equipment, or product system, whether acquired commercially off the shelf, modified, or customized, that is used to increase, maintain, or improve functional capacities of a child with a disability". The use of AT assists students in meeting the same outcomes as their peers. As an accommodation tool to help students access the curriculum, AT devices should also be used and available in the remote learning environment. AT includes a variety of no-tech (use of a pencil grip), low-tech (using closed captions when watching a video in class), and high-tech tools (Frequency Modulation (FM) Systems sending speech waves to hearing aids), ranging from no-cost options to more expensive options.

To ensure accommodations work in a remote learning environment, educators should know and understand all of the tools available to them and to students. Understanding the Present Level of Education Performance (PLEP A) within the IEP is the first step. The next step is to uncover any additional accommodations your students may need in the remote learning environment and create a plan on delivering the accommodations while not in school.

Depending on the need of the individual student, IEP, cognitive ability, and diagnosed disability will determine which of the most frequently used accommodations to use in the remote learning environment.

The Research

The distributed survey asked educators for success stories and suggested assistive technology resources to assist students with IEPs remotely. Frequently used accommodations fell into the following themes presentation, setting, response, and schedule/timing. The following strategies were identified throughout the research.

Presentation Accommodations

Presentation accommodations change the way the instruction, direction, and other information are presented to the students. Various presentation accommodations allow students to access information in various ways other than the standard means such as visual and auditory alone. Here is a list of the most common presentation accommodations on students' IEPs and related remote learning alternatives:

Advanced Graphic Organizers: Graphic organizers translated to the remote environment should be reasonably transferable by supplying students with electronic versions of the advanced graphic organizer. Canva.com is a website recommended by educators to create advanced graphic organizers to download and share with students.

Assistive Listening Device: Assistive listening devices, such as FM Systems, Loop Systems, Sound Field Systems, and Infrared Systems, which are supplied in school (in accordance with the students' IEP) to students to engage in classroom activities, should be provided remotely, if needed, to access the curriculum. All assistive listening devices may need to be delivered, mailed, or picked up, so the students have access to their required materials at home.

Audio Recordings: Synchronous lessons can be recorded and supplied for students. Additionally, NaturalReader.com offers free text-to-speech software, and Microsoft Learning Tools provides free immersive reader at onenote.com/learningtools.

Braille: Texts, workbooks, and all other resources that are supplied in Braille to the student at school (per the student's IEP) should be provided remotely for student use to access the curriculum in the remote environment.

Digital Text: While working with students remotely, provide the digital text as an alternative to written text.

Enlarged Print: Most computers, smartphones, and digital devices have built-in accessibility features to change the font size.

Frequent Breaks: When teaching a live streaming synchronous session, ensure there are allotted times for student breaks. If it would be too disruptive with a whole group meeting, perhaps allow students to chat message when they feel they need a break privately. Educators could also individually chat the students who need a break to remind them.

When lessons are asynchronous, frequent breaks should be posted on the individualized schedule so the student can independently move through the day and take their scheduled break. Timers could also be used to dictate when breaks should occur and when it is time to resume work. Educators could also embed brain break videos within digital assignments or include videos with exercises. Such videos can be found at GoNoodle videos, Koo Koo Kanga Roo, and KIDZ BOP.

Magnification Devices: Magnification devices, such as handheld magnifiers, video magnifiers, and screen magnifiers that are supplied in school (in accordance with the student's IEP) for students to engage in classroom activities, should be provided remotely, if needed, to access the curriculum. Additionally, most computers, smartphones, and digital devices have built-in accessibility features to change the font size and magnify the display.

Organized Materials: When working with students' parents to create a learning space, discuss the materials' organization, such as color-coding materials. For example, all materials associated with math are blue. Math materials include a blue notebook, blue folder, blue pencil case, etc. Only allow one color at the workspace at a time. It would be helpful to work with students to create a centralized location for all their materials.

Reader/Read Aloud Text: Text-to-speech software reads aloud words on computers, smartphones, and tablets and available on nearly every digital device. NaturalReader.com offers free text-to-speech software, and students can paste text or import documents into the tool, press play, and listen and read aloud. Students can also speed up or slow the reading speed.

Real-Time Captioning: Remote meeting platforms such as Zoom and Google Meets have real-time live captioning. Closed captioning is available for a video presentation for most video available through educator resource sites, YouTube, and TeacherTube.

Repeating Instruction/Recorded Instruction: In addition to NaturalReader.com (see Reader/Read Aloud Text), educators can record the assignment's instructions and send the recording to the student to replay. Most instructional videos can be recorded and replayed. When teaching an online session, record the session and provide the children access to view on their own time if they need to hear the instructions multiple times.

Simplified Instruction: Continue to have streamlined and concise instruction in the remote learning environment. Synchronously, supply simplified instruction using the private message chat tool to students. Asynchronously, provide simplified and straightforward written or recorded instructions.

Study Guides: Utilize US mail or email to supply study guides to students as needed.

Tactile Graphics: Tactile graphics, such as tactile pictures, maps, and graphs that are supplied in school (in accordance with the student's IEP) for students to engage in classroom activities, should be provided remotely or mailed to students, if needed, to access the curriculum.

Verbal or Visual Cues: While working with students remotely, continue to enhance instruction with verbal and visual cues throughout the lesson. Students will continue to benefit from visual instructions and cues throughout the lessons.

Written Instructions: Educators could schedule assignments to share and review before the lesson. Additionally, a concise, bulleted list of written instructions could also be posted in the chat feature during synchronous classes or provided directly on the assignments.

Setting Accommodations

Setting accommodations change various features and characteristics of the setting and allow for a change in the place, environment, or in how the environment is structured. Here is a list of the most common setting accommodations on students' IEPs and some remote learning alternatives:

Checklist of Needed Materials: During a synchronous lesson, a list of needed materials can be posted using the chat functions, or digital inventories of required materials can be shared with students before the class.

Flexible Seating: Flexible seating options can be used in a remote environment. While working with students or during weekly check-in with parents, suggest and explain available flexible seating options. For example, is there a counter that could be used as a standing desk? Maybe an ironing board can be set up for the correct standing desk height. Is there a stability ball available in the house to use as a chair? Is there a stool available for a backless chair? Is there a lap table to use while sitting on the ground while working? Are there egg crates available in the house? Knowing the student's individual needs based on IEP accommodations, most families have some options that they can use as flexible seating accommodations.

Quiet Space/Separate Room/Alternative Setting/Preferential Seating: Chunking these four frequently used accommodations together makes sense while remote learning. During your initial meeting with parents, discuss the home environment, and work together to create a plan to enforce the student's alternative setting and seating options. Consider a quiet space if an alternative setting is not possible. In that case, a homemade or store-bought study carrel along with noise-canceling headphones could give the same benefits as the quiet space, separate room, or alternative setting.

Reduced Noise/Distractions: A homemade or store-bought study carrel along with noise-canceling headphones could provide similar benefits as reduced noise and distractions.

Small Group or One-on-One Instruction: Small group and one-on-one instruction should continue in the remote learning environment through scheduled small group or individualized synchronous instruction through the video conferencing platform of choice. In addition to one-on-one video conferencing, educators could divide students into breakout rooms and conduct small groups or one-on-one instruction during the breakout session. Many educators note that they use paraprofessionals in breakout rooms to give students guidance in the small group setting or for one-on-one instruction.

Sensory Tools: Sensory tools can be replicated at home during remote learning. Most households have supplies that can be used to duplicate the type of sensory device the student needs. Examples of at-home sensory tools include Play-Doh, silly putty, slime, a little bowl of rice, Velcro strips, beads, and squishy toys. For fidgety legs and feet, an exercise band can be looped around the legs of the chair. Additionally, it may be beneficial to create a sensory toolkit using school supplies to be picked up or sent home with the student.

Sensory and motor paths can also be replicated at home. While meeting with parents, you could show them some examples of homemade sensory paths that could include hopscotch, wall jumps, long jumps, and have parents and students work together to create a sensory path outside or in a hallway to use during the day.

Response Accommodations

Response accommodations change how the student is required to respond and allow students to complete assignments and assessments in various ways other than just verbal and written responses. Here is a list of the most common response accommodations on students' IEPs and some remote learning alternatives:

Notetakers: While teaching a synchronous lesson through a video conferencing platform, record the class or use the video conferencing software to close caption, save, and transcribe the lesson. Most video tools will do all of the work for you. Another suggestion for remote learning accessibility is to suggest students play back the recorded lesson while using speech-to-text software. Also, save and share all presentations and PowerPoints with students.

Scribe: Speech-to-text software, such as Google Doc Voice Typing, will scribe and turn speech into text. Educators also recommend the audio feature in Flipgrid and dictation software in Microsoft Word.

Graphic Organizers: Send paper copies of graphic organizers home with students to complete assignments and assessments. Popplet.com, SpiderScribe.com, and Mindmeister.com are also recommended for student use in creating graphic organizers at home.

Augmentative and Alternative Communication (AAC) Devices: AAC devices, such as picture exchange communication systems, recorded speech devices, and electronic tablet speech applications, which are supplied in school for students to engage in classroom activities, should be provided remotely, if needed, to access the curriculum.

Appropriate Wait Time: During synchronous lessons, use appropriate wait times to allow students time to process questions and respond. Educators could also provide notes, presentations, and directions ahead of time and check in with students to answer any questions they may have.

Use of Visuals: Provide visuals throughout your synchronous and asynchronous lessons. Visual cues, such as pictures, photographs, and icons, can be used in digital instructions, assignments, and schedules. Additionally, most video conferencing platforms have whiteboard tools to use. Educators also recommend tools such as Jamboard to replicate a whiteboard by pulling images from Google searches, save work to the cloud, and draw and erase images. Bubbl.us is another tool recommended to organize educators' ideas visually in ways that make sense to students.

Calculators: Typically, calculators are built into computers, tablets, and smartphones for students to use in the remote environment. If a more complex calculator is required, the device can be sent home with the student to keep during remote learning.

Manipulatives: Educators can send home physical manipulatives from the school, use paper/printable manipulatives, or provide virtual manipulatives during remote learning. Recommended websites for virtual manipulatives are didax.com and mathplayground.com.

Oral Response: Students who have oral response accommodations as part of the IEP can respond, record, and send in the remote learning environment. Many educators recommend Flipgrid for students to use when recording themselves.

Spelling and Grammar Tools: Students who require spelling and grammar tools can access the same tools remotely through software such as Grammarly.com or use spell check in Google Docs and Microsoft Word.

Digital Pen: Digital pens that are supplied in school, following the student's IEP, for students to engage in classroom activities, should be provided remotely, if needed, to access the curriculum. The pens can be delivered, picked up, or sent home with students.

Schedule and Timing Accommodations

Schedule and timing accommodations change the amount of time or the schedule of instruction for the student. These types of accommodations allow for changes to when and how long a student has to complete tasks, assignments, or assessments and allow lessons to be broken down into smaller sections.

Extended Time for Tests/Multiple Testing Sessions: Break assessments down into sections by creating a Google Form for each section rather than assigning the test in its entirety. Have due dates for each section, and do not give more than one created portion at a time. Be flexible with due dates, and communicate with parents regarding the completion of each section.

Frequent Breaks: Schedule or embed time for breaks in the middle of independent assignments or break down tasks into smaller chunks of time to promote breaks. Have students use a kitchen timer or use free virtual countdown timers available, such as online-stopwatch.com.

Brief Assignment (or Broken Into Parts): Student assessments can be split into chunks, completed in sections, or over multiple days by creating multiple digital forms for each area or emailing students a section at a time to complete.

Visual Schedule: Visual schedules can be created and posted in the student's remote learning space. Such schedules can be made using picture exchange communication systems, photographs of students doing work, or icons representing each subject.

For students who may need extra support with the organization and executive functioning, color-coded posted schedules could help. Assign each subject area a color. As students work through the posted visual schedule, they can cover up the completed task or move a paper clip down the schedule to visualize completion and accomplishment.

Reduce Audio and Visual Overload: To reduce audio and visual overload, create, or have students purchase or borrow a study carrel while using noise-canceling headphones to complete a task, assignment, or assessment.

In conclusion, many accommodations can be replicated at home through educational technology, virtual applications, available household items, or various assistive technology options. Appendix 6.1 is a tracking sheet used as documentation and a reference when transferring at school accommodations into remote learning.

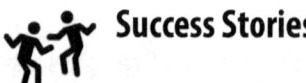

Success Stories

Stephanie, a special education teacher in South Carolina, creates accommodation binders for her students to access at home. She explains that since she has put together hands-on accommodation binders created specifically to each of her students' accommodation needs, she has noted significant gains in progress.

She suggests creating an individualized accommodation binder to each student's accommodation needs. The binder would contain each student's frequently used accommodations such as multiplication tables, a calculator, manipulatives, graphic organizers, visual communication flashcards, and other often used accommodations. The student can have easy access to the binder and independently learn when to access the needed accommodations when home. She creates these binders once a semester and has a drive by pickup time at the school. For those who do not show up, she will deliver or utilize her paraprofessional to deliver the materials to her students' homes.

Quick Tips From Educators

Louis, a special education administrator from Massachusetts, reminds educators to provide the same accommodations remotely that you would in school. Just think of alternative ideas they can be provided remotely – such as using breakout rooms for small group instruction and maybe providing close captions on live video instruction.

Mark, a special education middle school teacher from New Hampshire, suggests utilizing paraprofessionals to implement accommodations such as scribes during virtual instruction or having them create manipulatives, sentence strips, etc. to be sent home.

Brian, a special education teacher in Massachusetts, suggests visiting www.modmath.com. This app can be downloaded to provide virtual graph paper and pencil-free format to complete arithmetic designed for students with dyscalculia.

 Highlighted Resource

Bookshare is a no-cost assistive technology tool that benefits a wide variety of abilities and disabilities, such as, and not limited to, dyslexia, visual impaired, developmentally delayed, and intellectually impaired. The reading experience can be customized and includes audiobooks, highlighted text, Braille, large font, etc., and the tool also contains study tools and bookmarking. The website to access Bookshare is www.bookshare.org/cms/.

 Remember

- ✓ Accommodations and assistive technology (AT) are essential in the remote learning environment for students with IEPs.
- ✓ To make accommodations work in a remote learning environment, educators will need to know and understand their students' accommodations.
- ✓ Accommodations do not change what is being taught. Accommodations help students access the curriculum.
- ✓ Many accommodations, broken down by presentation, setting, response, and schedule, can be replicated at home.

- ✓ Presentation accommodations change the way the instruction, direction, and other information are presented to the student.
- ✓ Setting accommodations change various features and characteristics of the setting and allow for a change in the place, environment, or in how the environment is structured.
- ✓ Response accommodations change how the student is required to respond and allow students to complete assignments and assessments in various ways other than just verbal and written responses.
- ✓ Schedule and timing accommodations change the amount of time or the schedule of instruction for the student.
- ✓ All students who require accommodations listed on PLEP A or PLEP B of the IEP should be provided the same type of accommodations at home.
- ✓ The use of AT assists students in meeting the same outcomes as their peers. The use of AT devices as an accommodation tool helps students access the curriculum and should also be used and available in the remote learning environment.

6.1

Appendix: Sample Remote Accommodation Documentation

ABC School District

Remote Accommodation Success Tracker and Documentation

Student Name	
Date of Birth	
Parent/Guardian	
Parent/Guardian Contact Information	
Case Manager/Teacher	
Virtual Meeting Link (if needed)	

IEP Accommodation	Remote Equivalent	Parent/Caregiver Feedback *Include Date of Communication	Additional Notes and Action Items

References

Individuals with Disabilities Education Act. (2004). https://sites.ed.gov/idea/
Smith, D., Tyler, N., & Skow, K. (2018). *Introduction to contemporary special education: New horizons*. Pearson, New York, New York.

7

Synchronous Activities and Strategies

> *I have so many positive experiences to share about teaching my special education students remotely. My students are making tremendous growth in their IEP objectives. They are focused and eager to engage. I think it is because we enter our daily virtual meetings with fun – whether it be in costume, changing our screen names, wearing sunglasses, these extras make learning from a distance fun. I want them engaged and participating right from the beginning, and these activities are working!*
> *– Jennifer Thompson, K–2 Special Education Teacher*

In March 2020, most educators heard the term synchronous learning for the first time in their careers. Defined as the "interaction of participants with an instructor via the Web in real-time" (Khan, 2006), synchronous learning quickly became a significant challenge for educators across the country. After years of teaching, earning multiple degrees, and incorporating professional development hours, many would soon need to learn how to teach children with diagnosed disabilities – in real-time, over the Internet. And they must do so while continuing to adhere to all the IDEA laws, reinforce IEP goals and objectives, and provide appropriate accommodations. Educators across the country would need to learn how to pivot their teaching strategies into the unknown world of synchronous remote learning. That may sound daunting, but many educators are succeeding and are willing to share what works.

As educational leaders, teachers and service providers explore and learn the most effective way to educate remotely children with learning challenges and disabilities. Most research and literature on synchronous learning strategies for individuals with disabilities have focused on college-age individuals with minimal references to the K–12 educational landscape. In higher education, synchronous learning has been noted to provide instant feedback and interaction with classmates and educators, promoting engagement in an online learning environment (Falloon, 2011; Strang, 2013; Watts, 2016). Given the need for student engagement and social interactions, many school districts prefer synchronous methods over asynchronous ones.

The Research

This chapter's strategies are a collection of success stories and successful approaches by educators who teach children with disabilities and learning challenges remotely. Through trial and error, the dedicated educators working with students on IEPs share their successful strategies to promote engagement and learning objectives. Data were collected through the 257 participating educators in addition to interviews with select teachers, service providers, paraprofessionals, and administrators. One hundred percent of interview participants noted that synchronous teaching was the best delivery when teaching children with disabilities and learning challenges remotely. Furthermore, 90 percent of survey participants provided a synchronous success story when asked to "share a remote learning success story". Given this information, it seems that providing synchronous instruction is the preferred method to achieve IEP goals based on the study's collected input.

Synchronous Activities and Strategies

The following approaches were shared to create synchronous remote classrooms to improve remote learning for children with various disabilities and learning challenges. Here are some highlighted strategies:

Establish Classroom Rules

Whether teaching in an inclusion classroom, substantially separate room, or resources room, typically educators spend the first few weeks establishing rules, routines, and a sense of community. In the remote classroom, that should not change. Spend time at the beginning of the year to teach and create behavior expectations and remote learning etiquette. Although it is not recommended to create an overwhelming number of classroom rules, the survey results suggested rules essential for remote learning. Overall, some suggested remote learning rules that were shared throughout the survey results are highlighted next.

Example of Remote Classroom Rules

1. Be on time.
2. Find a quiet learning spot without distractions.
3. Behave the same way you would in school.
4. Mute yourself if you are not speaking.
5. No toys allowed while learning.
6. No phones or social media.
7. No pets are allowed while learning.
8. Dress up like you are in school.
9. Use the restroom before learning starts.
10. Raise your hand/use the raised hand key to speak.
11. Do not distract others.
12. Eat before learning starts.
13. Have materials close by and available.
14. Use headphones when possible.
15. Ask questions when you need help.

Class Constitution: Many educators suggest creating a classroom constitution. A classroom constitution helps students understand the importance of having rules to maintain order and have a voice in making the rules. Students feel a sense of ownership and accountability to follow the rules by allowing students to create remote learning environment rules.

Depending on the classroom size, this might be a whole group activity, or it could be done with partners or groups. Using the chosen video conferencing platform, have students work together or partner students using the breakout room tool. Have each group come up with five essential rules to follow in the remote environment.

Come together and discuss each group-suggested rule and use voting to select which ones to add to the constitution.

Once a classroom constitution is created, all students and their parents sign it and promise to follow the rules. As the educator, it is critical to create a visual of the rules established in the constitution and reinforce the rules each day before the lesson begins until they understand the remote classroom's expectations and etiquette.

Identifying five or six classroom rules is a good start to provide students a set of parameters for students to focus on without overwhelming them. Once the initial set of expectations is hardwired, educators can add additional rules and guidelines.

Post Remote Classroom Rules: Before learning activities begin, remind students of the remote classroom rules. Spending a few minutes regularly to review the rules is a good investment of time and energy. Show students the visual list or created constitution, and you might consider cutting and pasting the rules in the chat feature each day.

Consistent Predictable Schedules and Routine

Provide students with a predictable daily schedule. Keep the schedule consistent each day. Any deviations from the routine can create an opportunity to lose students and can cause frustration. Keep the day and schedule of synchronous classes and activities as predictable as possible.

Invite Other Teachers

Create opportunities for collaboration with the teachers who share the educational responsibilities of teaching students with IEPs. Develop synchronous experiences by inviting other teachers to join your remote class or ask to join theirs. General education teachers, special education teachers, and instructional assistants can create a richer, more meaningful educational experience for students on IEPs when working together and collaborating.

For example, instructional assistants and one-on-one aides can attend students' general education synchronous classes and report back to the special educator on the general education class objectives. In turn, the special educator can use that knowledge to create meaningful lesson plans incorporating the general education remote classroom activities in their synchronous class.

Therapy Co-treats

Service providers have noted the benefits of working together to create a predictable and consistent schedule to co-treat students remotely. Scheduling therapies, such as occupational therapy (OT), physical therapy (PT), and speech, have been challenging because many service providers have noted the absolute need for parent engagement for student safety and reinforcement. Asking parents to participate in these services daily is asking a lot for working parents. However, with co-treats, scheduling an extended session once a week makes it easier for parents to commit to once a week to help and assist service providers and their children.

An example of a co-treat activity could include creating a digital board game or scavenger hunt. For example, service providers have created digital board games for students to participate in. Each time they land on a space, the activity expected of the student varies. For example, students roll a die, and the space they land on could have them write their name (OT), say a nursery rhyme (speech), walk three stairs one foot at a time (PT), cut a straight line (OT), along with some preferred activities to keep student interest. Each time the students land on the spot, the activity changes.

Parents have told the service providers that they appreciate the co-treats and feel more involved now that they understand expectations.

Small-Group Instruction

Unless IEPs are modified through an IEP amendment due to remote learning, the service delivery of academic supports and other services listed on the students' IEPs should continue.

Students still benefit from one-on-one meetings or small group instruction. Legally, educators and service providers should continue to meet one-on-one with students to provide educational services as dictated by the IEP service grid in the remote environment.

In addition to IEP requirements and the legalities through IDEA (2004), one-on-one meetings are essential to keep students engaged and connected while teaching remotely. One-on-one sessions are an opportunity to take a learning and well-being inventory to determine how the students are doing academically and emotionally.

Start Meetings With a Fun Activity

Start each synchronous meeting with an engaging event to excite students to join before starting academics. For example, on Monday, have students wear a silly hat. On Tuesday, schedule a household scavenger hunt. On Wednesday, allow students to wear a costume to class. On Thursday, wear a crazy hat, and Fridays are show and tell. Such activities have students looking forward to attending, boost engagement, and increase participation (Welby, 2020). Figure 7.1 shows a teacher starting her synchronous class dressed as Funtime Freddy while holding a Bon Bon puppet. Starting the day with some fun will immediately engage students.

FIGURE 7.1 Teacher Dressed in a Mask in Front of a Computer

Five-Minute Rule

Teachers and service providers suggest a five-minute rule. Spend five minutes on an activity, then change the activity to keep students engaged and actively participating. Educators note that spending too long doing one thing has diminished engagement and retention on topics. Here is a sample five-minute rule agenda.

Five minutes – Teacher leads activity/discussion
Five minutes – Student discussion
Five minutes – Breakout rooms
Five minutes – Independent activity/media activity
five minutes – Regroup and repeat

It can be too easy to lose the interest of students. The five-minute rule has increased engagement, active listening, and participation in activities, especially for students with attention deficits, processing disorders, and retention difficulties. This strategy can be used in all classroom and OT, PT, speech, and social groups.

Boom Learning

Students with limited verbal skills or nonverbal have benefited and flourished from participating in Boom Learning activities. Boom Learning is a platform that permits educators to download free or paid digital activities for students of all ages, specializing in K–12 students. Boom "decks" are digital and made up of individual task cards for students to complete. Educators note that it is easy to differentiate instruction and activities to individualized student's needs. Boom Learning can be accessed at www.boomlearning.com.

Cue Cards and Flash Cards

Additionally, teachers have been sending home enlarged flashcards with symbols and cue cards to students with limited verbal skills or nonverbal. By using cards to communicate, teachers are able to keep students engaged, ask questions, and can measure understanding depending on the cards the student holds to the screen.

Transition Brain Break Videos

Breaks improve the mental ability and focus of students. Frequent physical movement breaks also allow students to regulate their behavior and emotions. When children must sit and remain in one place, it is likely to negatively affect fatigue and disruptive behavior (Levine, 2015; Brekke-Sisk, 2006). Incorporating movement breaks throughout the day can improve readiness to learn. Incorporating movement breaks routinely during the transition of activities prevents behavior incidents before they start. When transitioning between activities, use brain break videos such as GoNoodle, Koo Koo Kanga Roo, and KIDZ BOP. These suggested videos offer movement breaks, which include songs with movement, dance videos, and exercise routines.

Digital Think-Pair-Share

When conducting synchronous activities, use the same collaborative strategies that work in the classroom. For example, think-pair-shares are popular and used widely in classrooms as a peer collaboration strategy, especially in an inclusive environment with all ability levels. Luckily, most video conferencing platforms have tools to create breakout rooms.

While teaching synchronously, create opportunities to pause, think, and reflect on the topic discussed. Ask higher-order questions to promote the subject's application and allow students to work together to come up with an answer.

First (THINK), ask students a question and give the time and the opportunity to process the question and think of the answer independently. Second (PEER), using the breakout room tool creates partnerships and allows students to discuss possible responses. Create strategic partnerships based on the individualized needs and abilities of each student. Third (SHARE), end the breakout rooms and have all students share what was discussed in the breakout room. Not only does this strategy create opportunities for student interaction and engagement, but it also promotes student engagement within the synchronous remote environment.

Games and Challenges

Let's have some fun! Students love a little competition now and then. There are various apps to create opportunities for games during synchronous lessons.

For example, Kahoot.com is a game-based learning platform that educators can use to create trivia games for collaborative or independent fun during synchronous learning. Educators use Kahoot to reinforce the lesson taught and get a sense of class understanding of topics and have noted success among all ability levels.

Mixing Up Preferred and Non-Preferred Activities

IEP learning goals, benchmarks, and objectives may not be the student's preferred synchronous learning activity. Mixing preferred and non-preferred activities increase engagement, participation, and willingness to engage in those less desired activities. Individually tailoring the preferred activities to each student's interest had led to an increase in individual productivity.

For example, create popsicle sticks with a mix of preferred and non-preferred activities. Each popsicle stick should have a written-out activity to address an IEP goal or objective or an individualized preferred activity, such as show me your favorite toy or pet, or do a cartwheel. All popsicle sticks will be complete within the duration of the class or therapy session. When adding fun to activities, students are more willing to participate in the non-preferred activity. Wheeldecide.com is a website that can replicate this strategy digitally (Welby, 2020).

Additionally, Toytheater.com is an educator recommended website with a collection of interactive educational games for the remote learning classroom. Some activities, such as Balloon Pop or BINGO could be used as a preferred activity. Toytheater.com also has educational games that could align with IEP goals and objectives.

Emotional Check-Ins

Checking in with students while remote learning is more challenging than it was working with students in person. Check-in on students' emotional well-being can significantly affect relationships, communication, engagement, and learning. Here are two examples of how educators can take a quick inventory during synchronous learning:

Google Forms: Educators could create a daily Google Form with a straightforward question and multiple answers.
How are you doing today?

A. Happy
B. Calm
C. Ready to Learn
D. Sad
E. Frustrated
F. Worried
G. Mad

Students spend three seconds answering the question, and educators can spend three seconds looking at the responses. If there are any concerns, the educator can check in one-on-one with that student.

Private Chat: Another suggestion is using the private chat feature in the video conferencing platform; have students send an emoji of how they are feeling today. Again, follow up on the students who sent a concerning emoji.

Record Live Lessons

Teachers, administrators, and service delivery providers commented on the benefits of recording live instruction. Here are the benefits of recording live instruction:

1. Absent students can access video recordings.
2. Parents can refer to video recordings to learn difficult concepts.
3. Service providers such as occupational therapists, physical therapists, social-emotional specialists, and speech and language pathologists can share service delivery lessons

with parents so they can reiterate lesson concepts and objectives at home. They can also reuse some of the videos with other students, as long as students were not recorded, just the instruction.
4. Administrators also suggest that it has been helpful to view recorded live classes as part of the faculty evaluation process. Administrators note that this has helped them with their teacher evaluations and other monitoring and check-in requirements.

Most educators keep the recording in a classroom communication hub or platform such as Blackboard, Canvas, or Google Classroom. If it is an individualized lesson recorded for one student, educators have emailed them to students, and copied parents.

Work Together on Google Docs

Working together with students simultaneously on Google Docs can provide feedback in real-time. By doing this type of activity, students can transform their original work with more focus and accuracy. Educators report that this approach provides better insight into student learning and the ability to modify the assignments immediately. In many cases, it was reported that students get excited, and engagement increases when collaborating in this way.

Send Home Tools, Manipulatives, and Hard Copies

Many educators note the importance of sending home the materials they use for live instruction, such as manipulatives, sentence strips, occupational therapy tools, physical therapy apparatuses, speech flashcards, read-aloud books, and worksheets. Students can read, review, and learn from the hard copies of assignments along with the digital copies. Using the hard copies during synchronous activities has been useful in showing students how to do work or allowing them to work on hard copies as the teacher explains it digitally.

Virtual Clubs

Create a sense of belonging with virtual "clubs" using IEP goals and objectives as the focus. Calling small group instruction a "club" sounds more appealing to students than the leveled math group or reading group.

Create book clubs with multiple students based on their reading levels and similar IEP goals. Treat the book clubs as a social event and suggest that students come to these meetings with snacks and drinks. Add fun activities such as dramatic play where students can dress in character while engaging in comprehension activities or reading extension activities in addition to working on yearly IEP reading or comprehension goals (Welby, 2020).

Communication Tracker

Special education teachers and case managers speak to many different professionals and are ultimately responsible for their students' schedules and tracking of students' progress on their caseloads. Remote communication can get tricky to track and document. Appendix 7.1 is a sample communication tracker special education teachers and case managers can use to track conversations with therapists and outside agencies.

 **Success Story**

Diane, a high school intense needs/medical fragile, special education teacher from Massachusetts, has had remote successes teaching her students life skills.

In the remote classroom, Diane was able to teach one of her students how to shave, brush his teeth, do laundry, fold clothes, and hang up his shirt. It was an amazing transformation. Diane's student used the skills in his home and applied the learning to real-life rather than just the school lab classroom. The remote learning environment was beneficial for the application of life skills in the home environment.

 ## Quick Tips From Educators

Ellen, a K–2 special education teacher from Connecticut, recommends supplying students with worksheets in dry erase sleeves such as page protectors to use as a personal whiteboard. Students can show their work during synchronous activities. She also encourages parents to sit within earshot of her session to follow along with what is going on and can carry over the learning into the home environment.

Jennifer, a middle school special education teacher from Utah, suggests using a document camera to write, explain, and draw examples for students. Manipulatives are viewed similarly to how they would look and be used on the table next to them.

Jane, a K–1 teacher from Alaska, suggests hands-on activities remote instruction. This has provided her students with a fun and joyful experience with maximum engagement. Families can pick up materials from the school or the materials can be sent home before the scheduled lesson.

Lucy, a K–5 special education teacher in Massachusetts, recommends sending hard copies of all assignments home, along with learning tools like number lines, alphabet strips, and paper manipulatives. She also recommends making a copy for the educators. When teaching a lesson, use the hard copy to instruct while the students use their copy to learn. They can complete the assignment digitally or by hand – accept either copy.

 ## Highlighted Resource

MobyMax.com is a no-cost research-based online learning solution designed to provide kindergarten through eighth-grade common core standard aligned content, assessments, and activities that can be personalized for individual students. Currently, MobyMax covers over 25 subject areas, including the core subjects – math, reading, vocabulary, phonics, spelling, science, and social studies.

All possible IEP academic area content is covered. In addition to content, MobyMax provides a complete and customizable collection of formative and summative assessments, including benchmark assessments. Specifically, teachers have mentioned the benefits of using this program for remote IEP progress monitoring and assessment tracking. Educators assign standards that align with IEP goals and can track improvements and the percentage of accuracy. The educator can reassign tasks until students achieve the goal.

 Remember

- ✓ Spend time at the beginning of the year to teach and create behavior expectations and remote learning etiquette.
- ✓ Check in on students' emotional well-being because it can significantly affect relationships, communication, engagement, and learning.
- ✓ Provide students with a predictable daily schedule. Keep the schedule consistent each day.
- ✓ Unless IEPs are modified through an IEP amendment due to remote learning, the service delivery of academic supports and other services listed on the students' IEPs should continue regardless of delivery modality.
- ✓ Start each synchronous meeting with an engaging event to excite students to join before starting academics.
- ✓ Mixing preferred and non-preferred activities increase student engagement, participation, and willingness to participate in those less desired activities.
- ✓ Incorporating movement breaks throughout the day can improve students' readiness to learn.
- ✓ Service providers have noted the benefits of scheduling collaborative co-treat therapy sessions.
- ✓ Recording live sessions are beneficial.
- ✓ Send home the materials used for live instruction, such as manipulatives, sentence strips, occupational therapy tools, physical therapy apparatuses, speech flashcards, read-aloud books, and worksheets.

7.1

Appendix: Sample Case Manager Remote Communication Document

ABC School District

Case Manager Remote Communication Tracker

Student Name	
Date of Birth	
Case Manager/Special Education Teacher	
General Education Teacher	
Occupational Therapist	
Speech and Language Pathologist	
Physical Therapist	
Counselor/Social Worker	
BCBA/Behavior Therapist	
Other District Therapist	
Outside Service Providers	
Pre-determined Meeting Dates and Times	

Date of Communication	Virtual Communication	Spoke With	Notes and Actions Needed
	Email Phone Text Virtual Platform		
	Email Phone Text Virtual Platform		
	Email Phone Text Virtual Platform		
	Email Phone Text Virtual Platform		
	Email Phone Text Virtual Platform		

Synchronous Activities and Strategies ◆ 97

	Email Phone Text Virtual Platform	
	Email Phone Text Virtual Platform	

References

Brekke-Sisk, N. (2006). Standing-room only in classroom of the future. *Mayo Clinic Magazine*. Retrieved from https://mcforms.mayo.edu/mc4400-mc4499/mc4409-0906.pdf

Falloon, G. (2011). Making the connection: Moore's theory of transactional distance and its relevance to the use of a virtual classroom in postgraduate online teacher education. *Journal of Research on Technology*, *43*, 187–209. https://doi.org/10.1080/15391523.2011.10782569

Individuals with Disabilities Education Act. (2004). https://sites.ed.gov/idea/

Khan, B. H. (2006). *Flexible learning in an information society*. Hershey, PA: Information Science Publishing.

Levine, J. A. (2015). Sick of sitting. *Diabetologia*, *58*(8), 1751–1758. https://doi.org/10.1007/s00125-015-3624-6

Strang, K. (2013). Cooperative learning in graduate student projects: Comparing synchronous versus asynchronous collaboration. *Journal of Interactive Learning Research*, *24*, 447–464.

Watts, L. (2016). Synchronous and asynchronous communication in distance learning: A review of the literature. *Quarterly Review of Distance Education*, *17*(1), 23–32.

Welby, K. (2020). *How to improve distance learning for students with IEPs*. San Francisco, CA: Edutopia. Retrieved from www.edutopia.org/article/how-improve-distance-learning-students-ieps

8

Asynchronous Activities and Strategies

Easy to follow schedules are so important for asynchronous learning. Creating what we call a "hyperdoc schedule" has been working very well with a student who may have difficulty with executive functioning. A hyperdoc schedule is a daily schedule that students can follow independently. Each day all of their scheduling links are on one easy to navigate location. The hyperdoc contains classroom assignments for the day broken down by time, including movement breaks, specialist links, and related service provider links. Hyperdoc schedules keep students independently engaged and on track with minimal teacher interventions.

– Kellie Alessandro, Special Education Teacher

Some might think that creating independent asynchronous learning activities for students with learning challenges is an impossible feat, but outstanding educators across the country are proving the skeptics wrong. Through initial student coaching, parent support, and proper preparation, educators are making it happen – and surpassing expectations. Educators have found strategies to keep students with IEPs on task and achieve IEP goals with minimal teacher intervention during scheduled asynchronous learning time. While challenges exist, many educators have found strategies built on consistency and routine are effective at making asynchronous learning successful.

Asynchronous learning is another term K–12 educators did not hear much about prior to March 2020. Suddenly, educators are faced with creating asynchronous lessons along with their traditional, synchronous versions. Asynchronous learning, defined as "an interactive learning community that is not limited by time, place or the constraints of a classroom" (Mayadas, 1997), emphasizes flexible learning that students are not required to be online simultaneously and generally facilitated by emails and discussion boards (Hrastinski, 2008). This form of learning could take place on various learning platforms such as Canvas, Blackboard, or Google Classroom. Typically, the educator provides materials, such as assignments, recorded videos, self-guided lesson modules, prerecorded video instructions, and students completing their own time with expected due dates.

The Research

The importance of a consistent schedule was mentioned by over 75 percent of all participating educators, highlighting that the foundation of any successful strategy is an effective routine that their students can independently follow, especially during independent asynchronous activities. Children require consistency and routine, and it is critical for the success of asynchronous remote learning and the student's independence. Within survey and interview results, asynchronous seems to be the least preferred method to teach students with IEPs; most strategies share synchronous activities. However, the main takeaways are the importance of routine, clear expectations, and relationships. Strategies in this chapter are a collection of success stories and successful asynchronous approaches by educators.

Asynchronous Activities and Strategies

The following specific ideas were shared as effective asynchronous activities:

Find Opportunities to Connect
With fewer face-to-face interactions, developing and maintaining relationships with students becomes even more important than

usual. Find opportunities to connect with students – a quick phone call, an email to say hello, text message, a letter mailed to their house, a teacher parade, a video message to each student. Select one to three students a day and make an extra effort to connect with them while teaching asynchronously. Maintaining relationships and demonstrating that you care will go a long way in helping students achieve their learning goals.

Routines and Hyperdoc Schedules
Teachers referred to schedules and links embedded in documents as "hyperdocs" because it is a combination of all hyperlinks on one document in one place to make a schedule easily accessible to students. Therefore, teachers created the term hyperdoc (hyperlinks + documents = hyperdocs).

Instruction and schedules should be connected and organized with flow charts and embedded hyperlinks. Provide students with daily visual schedules that include times to work, embedded links to assignments, and movement breaks. Keep it simple and in one location to promote independence and consistency.

Hyperdoc schedules should contain all classroom activity links, brain breaks, live meetings, and service delivery links, all located on one daily document with highlighted times. More independent and older students can have hyperdoc schedules as checklists with times and daily links; younger students benefit from a visual schedule with icons and checkboxes with all hyperlinks embedded.

A daily Bitmoji classroom also proved successful. Linked within the Bitmoji classroom is the hyperdoc schedule checklist accessible to all students. The Bitmoji classroom was effective because it served as a visual guide for students who thrive with visuals.

Communicate Expectations
Create and communicate clear expectations for the asynchronous remote learning experience. If you are using a class remote platform such as PowerSchool, Canvas, or Blackboard, post asynchronous learning expectations within those systems. An effective approach is for educators to share expectations by posting weekly

or daily announcements that can be emailed or typed, an audio recording, or a video. Clear expectations prevent confusion. Some expectations posted could include:

- Daily schedule.
- Learning objectives.
- Weekly/daily learning goals.
- Rules and routine.
- Time expectations per subject.
- Daily service providers schedule.
- Due dates.
- Feedback.
- Contact information of everyone on the IEP team.
- Virtual office hours and links.

Post Daily Learning Objectives

Well-defined learning objectives are important because they provide students with a clear focus and purpose and leads to a feeling of accomplishment once achieved. Learning objectives should be posted in the remote classroom, communicated clearly, and reiterated consistently by teachers and parents.

Movement Breaks

Within the schedule, built-in movement breaks have been useful. Replicating the school's sensory-motor paths with a DIY sensory-motor path or suggesting students create one outside on a sidewalk or driveway with chalk is an excellent way to incorporate multiple movement breaks within the day. Here is an educator recommended link with free sensory path printables: www.weareteachers.com/wellness-way.

Recorded Videos

The use of recorded videos was mentioned frequently in the educator's survey. Although many of the video suggestions had different objectives, common themes and types of videos were daily welcome videos, weekly introduction videos, wrap-up videos, and instructional recorded videos.

Daily Welcome Video: Start each day with a daily welcome video highlighting activities and assignments for the day. Verbalize the daily learning objective and, depending on the age of students, read a book or tell them a story.

Weekly Introduction and Wrap-Up Video: Many educators noted the benefits of weekly introduction and weekly wrap-up videos to motivate students. Use these videos to set the stage and tone for what we are going to cover next and to wrap up and summarize what was learned that week.

Instructional Recorded Videos: When providing students with asynchronous learning programs, parents play a larger role in educating their children. To help reinforce content and IEP learning goals, record a mini-lesson including video instructions for students. By default, if students are struggling and need to ask parents for help, parents can refer to the video. Once everyone is on board and has access to recorded videos, educators should get fewer emails from both parents and students because video instructions are in a common place. Having video access helps parents understand expectations, reinforce learning goals, and can alleviate frustrations.

Create mini-lessons no longer than ten minutes. With short lessons, students and parents are more likely to watch them. Students with retention difficulties are more likely to retain the information by breaking up the task into pieces. Additionally, it will be easier to find specific topics students might need to be reinforced by having a shorter, more frequent instructional video to refer to. Some suggested video platforms are Panopto, Zoom, VoiceThread, and Flipgrid.

Morning Message Co-host

Collaborate with students on activities. For example, if you have a video recorded morning message or morning circle every morning, invite one student or two students a day to be your "co-host". Depending on the age and grade level, give your daily co-host a job. The student's job could be a daily weather reporter, sharing a news article, selecting a book, and reading it aloud to the class. Not only are you building a remote classroom community, but you are also connecting with at least one or two students a day.

GoGuardian
For a cost, many districts have opted to purchase GoGuardian to monitor and help students with asynchronous activities. GoGuardian is a tool designed to help teachers manage tablets, chrome books, and computer usage in their classrooms and monitor student activity on the device. The goal of the tool is to help keep students on-task and away from inappropriate content. If students cannot navigate something, regardless of location, educators can access their computer, Chromebook, or tablet and redirect or guide them. Teachers have noted that they can track students' activity during asynchronous activities and reengage or assist them if they are off track or cannot find an activity.

Resource Binders
Create monthly resource binders with all the hands-on activity, manipulatives, sentence strips, graphic organizers, multiplication tables, number lines, or any other materials used for accommodations. This binder is used as a student accessibility binder and should contain materials used for accommodation.

Model Expectations
During asynchronous activities, make sure students are provided with an end of activity model to replicate and understand expectations. Show your students what you would like the end result to look like. Modeling the expectations and final product can be shared during recorded lessons, emailed, or posted on the class page.

Group Work
Asynchronous learning can be isolating. Create activities that incorporate group projects and assignments that allow students to

work together. Working with their peers can minimize isolation, build community, and help build students' social and collaborative skills.

Add Incentives

Have some fun and increase engagement by incorporating incentives as a reward for completing independent assignments.

For example, Tracey, a Massachusetts kindergarten inclusion teacher, has been tasked with ensuring that each of her kindergarten students finishes ten minutes of *Lexia* a day during asynchronous learning time. Lexia is an independent virtual student-driven learning tool used to develop reading and language skills through individualized learning paths.

Each day, she gives her class a fun surprise incentive for each student who independently completes Lexia for ten minutes. The next time they meet remotely, she praises and follows through with her incentive promises. In Figure 8.1, Tracey promised she would place a bow on her head for each student who completed the assigned task.

Her students are excited about the fun incentive. By adding silly incentives, the teacher notes that independent participation increases, and students became more engaged and eager to complete directed tasks.

Gamification

Gamification is defined as the use of activities and external rewards to boost motivation in non-game contexts. Gamification intends to increase a person's experience and engagement in achieving a goal (Surendeleg, Murwa, Yun, & Kim, 2014). IEP goals are critical academic goals, and teachers have found that gamification makes it easy to track data and increases asynchronous participation leading to improved achievement.

Having fun with competitions is more comfortable when working synchronously on a virtual platform and can be more challenging when students independently complete assignments. For gamification to work, it must be simple and specific to your student's

FIGURE 8.1 Teacher with Bows for Each Assignment Completed by Students

needs. For example, give points for completing assignments and meeting objectives or following norms, rules, and remote procedures. Another example would turn lessons into quests, journeys, and scavenger hunts. Or possibly create specific individualized learning badges students can collect once IEP objectives and goals are met. In short, develop activities and incentivize what you would like your students to independently complete.

Frequent Formative Assessments

Frequent formative informal assessments in the remote learning environment are crucial to check for understanding and continuous progress monitoring for IEP objectives and benchmarks. Educators' opportunity to address misunderstandings is less frequent in an asynchronous classroom setup and can lead to students falling behind.

How you assign assessments should look different and be more frequent. For quick formative check-ins, educators can use Google Forms to check for understanding or use as a daily exit ticket for each class assignment. These assessments can also be conducted using online platforms such as Kahoot!, Socrative, or Padlet, which can each gather data for educator analysis and insight.

Students will require more frequent check-ins to ensure they are on the right track in achieving benchmarks and IEP goals. Without the day-to-day contact, checking in for understanding is imperative for students to attain their goals.

Provide Effective Feedback

More frequent assessments go hand and hand with providing useful feedback. With the increased number of formative assessments, students will need more feedback, which can be provided in one-on-one meetings, emails, phone calls, or online platforms. Flipgrid is ideal for younger students and Google Docs for older students, as effective means of providing feedback.

Rubrics

To avoid confusion, create clear and specific rubrics for the expectations of the assignment. Ensure students can view the rubric before beginning the assignment to understand what is required and the quality of what is needed. Depending on the cognitive ability and age of students, a visual-based rubric might be appropriate.

Virtual Office Hours

Hold virtual office hours once a week or once a day depending on availability. The virtual hours can be an opportunity for students to ask questions, discuss concerns or feedback, or share something that happened during their day.

Create a system to establish office hours. It could be an open Zoom or Google Meet link for students to drop in at any point. It could be a student sending a calendar invite. Or it could be a scheduled appointment. During asynchronous learning, students should have an opportunity to meet with their teachers, counselors, or service providers to ask questions.

Accept All Completed Work

Students come from different environments, and not all students have equal access to computers and tablets. Learning what works best for the family and accepting completed work through various methods such as electronic, picture texts, and paper copies have increased compliance and the frequency of completed work.

Flipped Classroom Approach

Some educators have found a flipped classroom approach works well to help students with IEPs during remote learning. This model blends elements of both the synchronous and asynchronous teaching models. For example, prior to delivering a live lesson using a video conferencing platform, educators send students prerecorded videos of lectures, instructions, slides, or a digital module to complete. The prerecorded asynchronous content is focused on student engagement and allowing students time to learn, explore, and apply the content. Synchronous class time is more focused on collaboration, discussion, and active learning, all of which increase interactions between the educator and students and peer interaction.

In addition to more interaction with students and more peer interactions, the flexibility allowed in the flipped classroom approach allows more time for educators to focus on the students who need additional support and has led to more flexibility in the differentiation of instruction. Students' time in breakout room discussion groups has allowed educators the extra time to work with students who require extra support or additional one-on-one or small group instruction.

Another noted benefit to the flipped classroom is the autonomy the students have over the pace of the instruction and availability to have the prerecorded video lectures to refer to if they are struggling.

Success Story

Alexandra, a high school special education teacher from Virginia, explained how asynchronous learning has been beneficial for many of her students, especially students with social anxiety. She predicts that graduation rates will increase with asynchronous learning options.

According to Alexandra, students who typically would have poor attendance, engagement, and participation are thriving with the option to check in each morning and then independently complete their work on their own time. Without all the external distractions and anxieties brought on during the in-person school day, many students complete their work successfully and submit it within outlined due dates.

Quick Tips From Educators

Alisha, a K–8 behavior specialist from Arizona, recommends creating a Bitmoji classroom with cool down corners visualized by pictures of bean bag chairs. If students click on the beanbags, there are options for sensory breaks, meditations, and brain break videos.

Katelyn, a high school special education teacher from Massachusetts, recommends keeping close track of daily asynchronous assignments. Whenever a student falls behind, email the student but copy the parent immediately. This shows the parents that you hold the student primarily accountable while keeping parents in the loop about what is going on in class.

Brian, an elementary special education teacher from Louisiana, recommends creating and sending home a sensory toolkit for students to access during independent activities. He used pencil cases and filled them with putty, chew tools, fidgets, gum, mints, mini stress balls, and a positive handwritten letter.

 Highlighted Resource

ReadWorks is used by special education teachers and reading specialists as a remote learning tool to differentiate instruction while focusing on IEP goals. ReadWorks is a free resource for all K–12 teachers that provides reading comprehension lesson plans. As a remote classroom tool, this is an online resource for reading passages to improve student reading comprehension skills by using the latest in literacy teaching research. The resource includes pre-made worksheets, quizzes, and other printable materials to supplement and enhance the lesson. These readings include both fiction and nonfiction passages and are sortable by keywords, grade or Lexile levels, or by a specific skill or strategy. Teachers can differentiate instruction based on students' ability levels and sort by students' comprehension IEP goals, for example, cause and effect, and lessons are generated specific to that topic, and Lexile entered. Additionally, teachers can print materials or maintain a virtual "binder" full of the materials they have used and provide comments on individual materials. The resource is found at www.readworks.org.

 Remember

✓ Create clear expectations for the asynchronous remote learning experience and communicate those expectations in writing.
✓ Keep schedules and assignments in one centralized location.

- ✓ Developing and maintaining relationships with students is important. Find opportunities to connect with students.
- ✓ Communicate your availability with students. Students should know how and when to reach you.
- ✓ Frequent formative informal assessments are crucial to check for understanding and continuous progress monitoring for IEP goals and benchmarks.
- ✓ Use rubrics and provide useful feedback so expectations are clear, specific, and concise.
- ✓ Working on a team project can minimize the feeling of isolation, build community, and help social and collaborative skills. Include group work with asynchronous learning.

References

Hrastinski, S. (2008). Asynchronous and synchronous e-learning. *Educause Quarterly, 31*(4), 51–55.

Mayadas, F. (1997). Asynchronous learning networks: A Sloan Foundation perspective. *Journal of Asynchronous Learning Networks, 1*(1), 1–16. https://doi.org/10.24059/olj.v1i1.1941

Surendeleg, G., Murwa, V., Yun, H., & Kim, Y. S. (2014). The role of gamification in education: A literature review. *Contemporary Engineering Sciences, 7*(29), 1609–1616. https://doi.org/10.12988/ces.2014.411217

9

Paraprofessionals and Remote Learning

Although working remotely has been challenging, it has forced me to be creative in establishing relationships with my students and the teachers I work with. Through my daily contact with students, I have observed just how truly resilient the students are and how quickly they can adapt from in-person to remote learning.

– Kellie Caffrey, Paraprofessional

Special education teachers – what would we do without paraprofessionals? Honestly, their role is essential to a special education classroom's success, and teachers would be lost without them!

Paraprofessionals, also known as program assistants, instructional assistants, teaching assistants, and teachers' aides, are critical to a special education classroom's success. Regardless of the type of classroom (inclusion, co-taught, resource room, or substantially separate and now remote), the paraprofessional has an essential role and greatly influences students' education. Paraprofessionals typically have a hands-on role with students with IEPs throughout the day and focus on support in the classroom, during services such as occupational therapy, physical therapy, and speech and language therapy; recess activities; and unified art subjects. Additionally, paraprofessionals work in small groups to reinforce IEP goals and learning objectives or work one-on-one with students focusing on learning, behaviors, and transitions.

There are many ways the paraprofessional can and should continue to provide support to students, teachers, and programs when schools transition to remote learning. Throughout the transition, supporting the teacher is essential to the consistency of the programming and students' success with IEPs.

The Research

Due to teacher shortages, many paraprofessionals have been pulled away from their classroom to substitute remotely for teachers. While some districts do not use assistants, others eliminated their use because of budget cuts or layoffs. In the survey, not all participants used paraprofessionals, but those who did mention their countless benefits. The survey showed that 47 percent (121 of the 257) of educators had a paraprofessional as support. An additional 15 educators who took the survey are paraprofessionals. In total, 136 educators share how teachers utilize paraprofessionals to enhance synchronous and asynchronous remote learning experiences. The following strategies were collected through the survey participants.

Strategies to Utilize Paraprofessionals in the Remote Classroom

Paraprofessionals are utilized from the class preparation process to IEP service delivery follow- through and everything in between. Here are some suggested strategies to utilize paraprofessionals in the remote learning environment:

Platform Management
Teachers mentioned the benefits of having paraprofessionals manage asynchronous and synchronous platforms while the teacher controls the classes' content, instruction, and assignments.

For example, in the asynchronous classroom, paraprofessionals can monitor the school's chosen platform, such as Blackboard or Canvas, by tracking the student submissions and discussion boards and alerting the teacher of any difficulties, missed assignments, or struggles students have.

During synchronous meetings, paraprofessionals can take attendance, monitor the chat feature in the chosen virtual conferencing platforms, such as Zoom and Google Meets. They can monitor student engagement and understanding of concepts that are being taught by teachers. Paraprofessionals can also help breakout room activities with students with IEPs and hold small group instruction in a breakout room for the students who need extra support.

Access to General Education Remote Platforms
When given access to the general education remote platforms, paraprofessionals can monitor the academic content taught in the general education classroom. By observing what is taught and how the students with IEPs are progressing, they can report to the special education teacher or case manager on individualized student needs.

Create a Virtual Library
Teachers have utilized paraprofessionals to record a daily read-aloud or create a virtual library of age-appropriate read-alouds. The book is chosen based on students' IEP needs or for whole-class activities. After a virtual library is completed, the teacher has various books and genres to choose from, whether the goals are a whole class book for enjoyment or an individualized IEP goal. Regardless of how the teacher decides to utilize the virtual library, having various books available saves time.

Life Skill Videos
Many students with IEPs have life skill goals to promote independence and independent living. Teachers have worked with paraprofessionals to create videos highlighting different life skill objectives for individualized student needs from washing hands through job interviews. Students can watch and discuss videos during asynchronous or synchronous meetings.

Attend General Education Classes
Most students with IEPs will spend most of their day in their least restrictive environment, which is the general education remote classroom. In the remote environment, common planning time between the general education teacher and special education teacher may not be as convenient or nonexistent, leaving most planning during personal time or after school. Having the paraprofessional act as the "middleman" between the two teachers has proven to be successful. When the paraprofessionals can attend the general education classroom, they can report back to the special education teacher the concepts taught and the learning objectives. Knowing what was taught can help the special education teacher create and plan upcoming lessons modifying the general education objectives and creating a parallel plan based on students' IEP goals and needs.

One-on-One Instruction and Small Group Instruction
Using the breakout room feature on a virtual conferencing platform or scheduling a specific time each day, paraprofessionals can work with students one-on-one or in small groups, focusing on reinforcing the special education teacher or general education teacher's lessons. The scheduled one-on-one time could also be an opportunity for a behavior check-in, social-emotional reinforcement, or a chance to do some progress monitoring.

Social Groups
Utilizing paraprofessionals to create social groups for students has worked well for teachers. During the social groups, the paraprofessional monitors social interactions and introduces some nonacademic fun by creating a dialogue between students, playing games, engaging students in scavenger hunts, and filling the social void that remote learning tends to generate.

Assist and Collect Materials
Remote learning tends to involve the dispersion of materials. Depending on access to the Internet, students' learning preferences

could include paper copies of all remote assignments. Organizing and distributing daily materials is a time-consuming task. Special education teachers report that they have a system that utilizes the paraprofessional to organize and distribute daily or weekly materials. Some districts utilize the paraprofessional to drop the materials at the home of the student. The drop-offs are usually contactless, leaving the packets in the mailbox.

Assistive Technology Assistance
Preparing and educating parents on assistive technology devices in the remote setting can be time-consuming. Low-tech assistive technology used in the remote learning environment includes graphic organizers, visual schedules, math manipulatives, pencil grips, slant board, adapted pencil, and writing materials. High-tech assistive technology used in the remote learning environment includes augmentative and alternative communication devices, screen magnifiers, mouse alternatives, voice recognition, and optical character recognition. Paraprofessionals have been utilized in multiple ways to facilitate in using assistive technology, such as helping families learn and assist their children with high-tech assistive technology devices and answering any questions families may have.

Research
Case managers and special education teachers have utilized paraprofessionals to research different types of lessons to help achieve students' specific IEP goals.

For example, a special education teacher creates a Google Doc with a list of all her students' IEP objectives. The paraprofessional then adds researched websites, documents, and literature that focuses on the teacher's objective to reference as they were lesson planning. Teachers can refer back to this document when planning future classes or small group instruction.

Send Letters to Students
Many teachers have been mailing students handwritten letters, cards, or quick notes to create a personalized experience while

promoting community and relationship building. Teachers mention that paraprofessionals have been taking on and following through with that initiative.

Service Delivery
Paraprofessionals have been used in various capacities by service providers, such as physical therapists, speech and language pathologists, and occupational therapists, while remote learning.

Paraprofessionals act to reinforce the services in several ways. Paraprofessionals have been participating and observing the service provider's sessions to support objectives throughout the day and week. Depending on district rules, policies, and expectations, some service providers work remotely while students are in school. Paraprofessionals have assisted the service provider by working in person with the student while the service provider instructs and explains activities virtually. Additionally, paraprofessionals have facilitated the communication between teachers and service providers, keeping the schedules intact.

Professional Development
While remote learning, paraprofessionals have the added responsibility to participate in professional development regarding remote learning instruction and expectations. Participating in professional development, they can learn new skills to help maintain the remote learning classroom.

Be a Buddy
Paraprofessionals have been assigned as social-emotional buddies for selected students to check in with. Students who need the extra social-emotional support that a teacher or caseworker cannot provide have been paired with a paraprofessional to act as a buddy or a sounding board if there are any needs.

Emotional Inventory
During instruction or morning meeting times, have the paraprofessional take an emotional inventory of students. Emotional inventory

can be accomplished through private chats. For example, students can privately send the paraprofessional a daily emoji of how they feel and, in turn, can keep the teacher aware of students' feelings and follow up with any concerns.

Develop Graphic Organizers
Depending on accommodations outlines in student's IEPs, some students require graphic organizers, advanced graphic organizers, or modified graphic organizers. Paraprofessionals have been utilized to research beneficial graphic organizers based on students' needs and modify existing graphic organizers.

Reteach, Repeat, Clarify, and Break Down Instructions
Many students with IEP have the accommodation to reteach instructions, repeat instructions, clarify instructions, or break down instructions into smaller parts. Paraprofessionals can provide this accommodation in a breakout session, in a one-on-one scheduled session, or through a recorded video that can be provided to the student.

Notetaking
Many students with IEPs have the accommodation to provide a notetaker. Paraprofessionals can provide this accommodation by attending virtual classes and share with students through the digital text.

Progress Monitor
Paraprofessionals can record student behavior observations during virtual classes. Additionally, they can keep anecdotal feedback of students' success and challenges as they work with students one-on-one or in small groups. They can share with the special education teachers or case managers to use during parent check-ins by documenting progress and monitoring behaviors.

Appendix 9.1 provides a sample student progress monitor documentation sheet that can be shared through Google Document so teachers and paraprofessionals can view in real time when needed.

Survey Needs

Paraprofessionals suggest that teachers should survey or check in with them frequently to gauge their professional development needs and their understanding and expectations of the job. Some felt that they could be doing more to assist the teacher, while others thought they were going way above and beyond. Working remotely and communicating digitally can lead to miscommunication and various misunderstandings in the remote landscape. Communication and mutual openness are essential in all relationships, including the professional relationship between the paraprofessional and the teacher.

Communication Template

Communication between the paraprofessional and the cooperating teacher can sometimes get overlooked with all the demands of remote learning. Appendix 9.2 has a sample communication tracking sheet that can be created on a Google Document and shared and updated in real-time. The ideas mentioned earlier and tasks can be documented in the communication sheet and be referred to as needed.

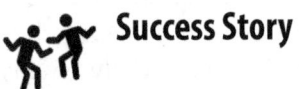

Success Story

Mari, a fourth-grade special education teacher from Georgia, utilizes her paraprofessional during morning meetings to take notes on "personal shares" to combine every Friday for gameplay and community building.

Every morning Mari has a morning meeting, and students share fun facts about themselves. For example, on Mondays, they share what they did that weekend. Tuesday, students share a story about a special person. Wednesday, students describe their favorite foods. Fun fact sharing happens daily for about ten minutes. While sharing, Mari's paraprofessional is jotting down the student's daily responses and, by Friday, combines all the answers to create a trivia game through Kahoot! The questions are all the personal shares of the week. A sample question could be, "Which one of your classmates went to Florida last weekend to swim at their Grandparent's house?" Students have a choice of four classmates and input their answers.

Mari has found that students look forward to the weekly Friday trivia game. The activity builds class community, reinforces relationships, helps social skills, increases verbal communication, and promotes listening skills. She also mentioned that this activity had increased engagement and class participation because students are excited to share with hopes their names will be displayed on the trivia game on Friday. Mari mentioned there was no way she could create such a fun event without her paraprofessional.

 **Quick Tips From Educators**

William, a paraprofessional from California, recommends regular check-ins and open communication with the partnering special education teacher or case manager. He thought he was not doing enough to support the special education teacher and the special education teacher felt like she was piling on too much work. With scheduled weekly check-ins, they now have better communication.

Jillian, a high school special education teacher from Massachusetts, suggests having paraprofessionals send students daily emails to remind them of the day's work expectations and who and how to reach out for additional support.

 Highlighted Resource

Wayne RESA is a regional educational agency that provides wide-ranging services and support to Wayne County's 33 school districts in Michigan. The agency's goal is to improve student achievement. Wayne RESA provides a wide variety of free useful tools for paraprofessionals such as training modules that focus on person-first language and conflict resolution and guidebooks to help paraprofessionals understand a variety of disabilities. It also provides already created data collection forms, training videos, and many more helpful resources and guides that can be found here: www.resa.net/teaching-learning/special-education/independence-paraprofessionals/paraprofessionals-resources

 Remember

- ✓ Paraprofessionals are critical to a special education classroom's success. Regardless of the type of classroom, the paraprofessional has an essential role and greatly influences students' education.
- ✓ Paraprofessionals can assist teachers during synchronous and asynchronous learning activities.
- ✓ Paraprofessionals can help students with accommodations outlined on the IEP, such as notetaking, breaking down instructions, clarifying materials, and reteaching.
- ✓ Paraprofessionals can maintain and update the virtual platform.
- ✓ Paraprofessionals can act as the middle person between the general education classroom and the special education classroom by communicating students' objectives, goals, assignments, and behaviors.
- ✓ Communication between the teacher and paraprofessional is important to ensure they are in sync with the students' needs.
- ✓ It is important to talk or survey a paraprofessional during remote learning because times can get busy. If there is a problem or miscommunication, it is best to know immediately.
- ✓ Tracking communication and tasks are important to document in the remote environment because days can get busy, and communication can be difficult.

9.1

Appendix: Sample Remote IEP Progress Monitor Tracking – Paraprofessional

ABC School District

Paraprofessional Remote Student Progress Monitor and Tracking

Note – paraprofessional progress monitoring and tracking is to be used as anecdotal data to assist the case manager/teacher in the remote classroom.

Student Name				
Date				
IEP Goal or Focused Objective				
Observation Documented By				
Location of Observation/Collected Data (Circle One)	Whole Group Virtual Platform	Small Group Virtual Platform	One-on-One	Other (Explain):
Observation Notes and Collected Data				
Case Manager/Teacher Signature				

Student Name	
Date	
IEP Goal or Focused Objective	
Observation Documented by	
Location of Observation/Collected Data (Circle One)	Whole Group Virtual Platform / Small Group Virtual Platform / One-on-One / Other (Explain):
Observation Notes and Collected Data	
Case Manager/Teacher Signature	

Student Name	
Date	
IEP Goal or Focused Objective	
Observation Documented by	
Location of Observation/Collected Data (Circle One)	Whole Group Virtual Platform / Small Group Virtual Platform / One-on-One / Other (Explain):
Observation Notes and Collected Data	
Case Manager/Teacher Signature	

9.2

Appendix: Sample Paraprofessional and Teacher Remote Communication Document

ABC School District

Teacher and Paraprofessional Remote Communication Document

Teacher	
Paraprofessional	
Scheduled Meeting and Planning Times	
Meeting Link	
Academic Year	

Date	Discussion	Action Items	Targeted Date of Action or Due Dates

10

Tips and Tools to Share With Parents

As I round the bottom of the stairs to meet my five-year-old son Jack, I pause and take a few deep breaths. As I have learned over the recent months, Jack feeds off my energy when I work with him. If I am stressed or anxious, so is Jack. If I am impatient or tired, so is Jack. If I am calm and happy, so is Jack.

– Vanessa France, Jack's Mom

As a result of the 2020 global pandemic, caregivers who have children with learning challenges, diagnosed disabilities, and exceptionalities have been asked to do the nearly impossible – teach their children while maintaining their home, multiple children's schooling, and their employment responsibilities. Parents are concerned about the logistics of the task and the fear of their children falling behind academically and missing developmental milestones while losing the life skills necessary for independent living. This chapter will explore a parent's perspective, some available research and survey results, and tricks and tools educators can share with parents.

Throughout the chapters, there was such an emphasis on parental expectations and involvement that I decided to fully understand their obstacles and challenges. Vanessa's story will provide further perspective along with some tools discussed throughout the chapters that can work at home with students.

A Parent's Perspective – Vanessa's Story

Vanessa France, a New England Mom and working professional, is trying to continue her career from home while her four young children learn remotely. As you imagine, she is faced with an incredibly daunting feat. Not only is Vanessa overwhelmed with her four children collectively engaged in remote learning, Vanessa's youngest child, Jack (age 5), has autism and has an Individualized Education Program. Like many parents across the county, Vanessa struggles to do it all and has countless concerns about Jack's progress.

At times, as educators, we can get so preoccupied with data collection, schedules, and creating the perfect lesson that we may forget to pause and reflect on the hardship parents are experiencing day to day. To get a glimpse into Vanessa's day, she and I had multiple conversations. Her perspective and insight were so real and powerful that I had to ask for her permission to share her story and perspective.

Here is Vanessa's story.

Jack

I ran from bedroom to bedroom upstairs to ensure my three older children were logged in to their proper online classes with no issues. I glance at the clock before heading down to log on with my youngest – I have 5 minutes before his virtual Kindergarten class starts and 35 minutes before my first of many conference calls for my job.

As I round the bottom of the stairs to meet my 5-year-old son Jack, I pause and take a few deep breaths. As I have learned over the recent months, Jack feeds off my energy when I work with him. If I am stressed or anxious, so is Jack. If I am impatient or tired, so is Jack. If I am calm and happy, so is Jack.

These unprecedented times have certainly put me to the test. Honestly, it has been a struggle to put on a happy face and remain positive for my children, especially for my youngest, Jack.

You see, my son Jack has Autism. To say it has been difficult taking on the role of not only his mom during this pandemic but now one of his teachers while virtually learning at home would be a complete understatement.

Jack doesn't learn like your typical student. Jack is on an IEP. The plan is designed specifically for Jack – catered in every way to his specific strengths and weaknesses.

His team of teachers and many specialists, such as an occupational therapist and a speech and language therapist, have been nothing short of incredible the entire time. However, there are a few things I wish I had realized in the beginning when I began working remotely with our son, but I am so very glad I do now as they have made our life less stressful. Here are some essential insights I would love to share with educators from my experiences and perspective. I want educators and other parents to know that it is OK to cross barriers, flexibility is important, and take it one day at a time!

Understandings From a Parent to Educators

1. Barriers May Be Crossed, and That Is OK

Times are stressful. We are in the middle of a pandemic, and it is exhausting for everyone – parents, teachers, students, and all of us. Sometimes, it is just too difficult to pretend everything is okay and going smoothly.

I remember the first time I lost it on a video call with one of the kid's teachers and broke down in tears. I felt so awkward; I felt I had just crossed a barrier. However, as I tried to hide the tears, I looked up to only realize the teacher was wiping away her own tears. She was a working mom too, and completely related to the stress I was under and felt it herself. At that moment, we were two stressed, worn out moms who just needed a good cry and a shoulder to lean on. And that's exactly what we did in that session. It was okay to let our guards down and be real. I gained much more respect for her and realized we are all just doing our best to get through this, and we can be honest about that, together. After that session, we were able to open up more and communicate on a whole new level for the betterment of my son.

2. Flexibility Is Important

IEPs are designed for in-school learning, and the same plan most likely will not work for virtual learning. When you have a specific plan designed for the "normal" in-person school days and suddenly try to implement that plan to virtual learning, it is just not going to work the same. There will be adjustments, and we all need to be okay with that.

Parents will try what they can at home, and if it doesn't work, that's okay – make the temporary changes as needed and keep communicating with the IEP team about what is working and what is not. Continue to adjust as needed. Flexibility is key.

3. Take It Day by Day

What may work today may not tomorrow. And that's okay. I remember struggling with Jack during his Unified Arts/Special Classes, especially Physical Education.

Jack simply did not enjoy watching other classmates dancing on the computer and did not want to dance with classmates watching him. I tried everything I could think of to make it fun for him and get him involved. I was beating myself up when I kept failing class after class after class. The struggle was all-consuming and heart wrenching. I finally brought this up to his Special Education Teacher, who simply said, "Okay, so if he doesn't want to do the dances while on video, just join in the beginning to say hello and end the virtual class whenever you need to. Then, do the dances/activities with Jack yourself, off the screen. Just do what works for him". Those last six words have been ingrained in my mind ever since – Just do what works for HIM.

Jack is on an IEP for specific reasons – the norm, the typical, the standard just doesn't work for my son. He needs a program that works for HIM. When things are upside down, stressful, and unknown, as a team, we need to focus on what works for him.

Vanessa's Final Thought

I have always had the utmost respect for teachers. As a family, after what we have been through over the past year, that respect has grown tremendously. And I don't think I am alone here. I think you will find this to be the case among the majority of families out there.

Working with children that have an IEP is no easy feat. Add a pandemic and a schedule that is flipped upside down, and that daunting task can sometimes feel overwhelming and impossible.

Educators' patience, resilience, strength, adaptability, and passion for educating have all been put to the test. Every single one of them not only stepped up to the plate, ready to take on the unknown, but they have all gone above and beyond for our children.

For that, I am immensely grateful.

– Vanessa France

Vanessa is not alone in the struggle. Every family I spoke to feels similarly. The struggle has been all-consuming, but the more the families educate themselves on what works for their child, the easier remote learning is becoming. As Vanessa stated, the norm, the typical, and the standard did not work for Jack. Understanding that the standard needs to be modified and individualized is essential in helping their children become successful remote learners. Ideas to share with parents will be shared in hopes to help parents navigate the remote learning landscape in their homes.

The Research

Across the country, various stakeholders have surveyed parents.

One highlighted study was through the Rhode Island Parent Information Network (RIPIN, 2020). RIPIN conducted an online survey of 427 parents with children who attend school in Rhode Island and receive special education services, and 82 percent of parents responded that their children need their help and support all or most of the time when the school districts switched to remote learning.

An additional investigation conducted through ParentsTogether Action in New York (2020) released results collected from a survey of 1,500 families around the US. The survey revealed that 80 percent of families who have children with IEPs report that their child is not receiving the appropriate supports outlined in the IEP, and almost 40 percent are not receiving any support. Additionally, the survey reported that parents with children working remotely with IEPs are twice as likely to say that distance learning is going poorly than for those without IEPs. Furthermore, media outlets report (Jacobson, 2020; Kamentz, 2020) that families file legal complaints that schools need to do a better job addressing their children's needs.

In combination with the multiple surveys that have been disseminated throughout the country and the media reports, there is no denying the predicament – parents are struggling to help their children with IEPs. Bottom line: Educating children with disabilities and learning challenges at home without in-person support has been challenging. Here are a few of the strategies discussed throughout the guidebook that could help parents.

Strategies and Tips to Share With Parents

Throughout the different chapters, some of the following suggestions were discussed that include specific focal points to share with parents and caregivers as we all work together to focus on the child's success.

Learning Space

Educators note that parents appreciate their input and recommendations in creating an at-home learning space to study and attend virtual sessions during remote learning. Working with parents to create an uncluttered learning space with visible schedules and easy to access learning tools are essential ways to partner in the initial stage of remote learning. Educators may also want to suggest good lighting and a comfortable workspace and chair. Additionally, the child may want to add some individual touches to the space to create motivation and inspiration, such as artwork and pictures.

Educators may want to provide parents literature or a quick tutorial video on flexible seating benefits and explain flexible seating options at home. Sitting for prolonged periods without movement or flexibility is not sufficient and can lead to health problems (Levine, 2015). Depending on the students' individualized needs and accommodations listed on their IEPs, educators may want to discuss some flexible seating options available in the home. Options could include using standing desks, using an ironing board at the proper height for their child to work on a counter-height table, or sitting on a stability ball at a desk. Other flexible seating options could be a backless seat such as a stool, adding resistance bands between chair legs to allow fidgety feet to move, or sitting on the floor with a lap table while learning and working.

Flexible seating gives students options for controlling their physical environment in ways that work best for themselves and their learning. Often with choices, students gain greater flexibility and control, giving them the autonomy and comfort to stay engaged and focused for more extended periods, overall leading to improved behavior, focus, and willingness to complete desired tasks. Figure 10.1 shows two examples of flexible seating. Using an ironing board for a standing desk or sitting on a stability ball are appropriate flexible seating options depending on the child's needs.

Additionally, when working with parents creating the learning space, this is an excellent opportunity to discuss limiting distractions. Removing technology that has access to social media and storing phones away from the child during school hours is helpful for older children.

FIGURE 10.1 Two Examples of Flexible Seating

Establish a Consistent Schedule

One of the most critical pieces in creating a successful remote classroom is a consistent, predictable daily schedule. A consistent schedule is comforting, and it can increase focus and willingness to work, especially in inconsistent times and environments, while transitions and schedule changes can add stress and lead to frustration and anger. Include parents in the design of a daily schedule. When creating the schedule, use pictures, graphics, and icons to make a child's visual schedule to follow.

Educators and parents should collaborate in creating schedules to create a visual and predictable daily routine. The child should participate in creating a plan to encourage independence and ownership of the daily routine. The schedule should be the same each day and posted in the designed learning space. Two specific strategies are suggested here:

Color-Coded Schedules – For students who may need extra support with the organization and executive functioning, color-coded posted schedules could help. Assign each subject area a color. For example, Science is blue on the daily schedule, and the science notebook and folder are all blue. Working with parents to organize subjects into colors will promote independence, ease transitions, and help independently organize the student's workspace. With practice and the daily routine, students will know to allow only one color in their workspace at a time. As each subject is completed, the color-coded material should be removed. As students work through the posted daily schedule, they can cover up the completed task or move a paper clip down the schedule to visualize completion and accomplishment.

First Then Chart – Depending on the student's need and ability levels, some students may not be ready to follow a posted schedule and may need tasks broken down with an immediate award. The suggested strategy is a "first then" chart.

A "first then" chart is a visual strategy to help students complete a specific, non-preferred task. The chart displays two pictures side by side. The "first" is a picture of the student doing schoolwork (the non-preferred activity), and the "then" is a picture of the student participating in a preferred activity (playing on the swings, etc.). The student must get through the "first" to earn the "then". When establishing remote learning routines, suggest parents take a picture of their child participating in each subject and use those pictures to build their schedule ("first"). As they complete each assignment on time, they earn a preferred activity ("then").

The following (Figure 10.2) shows a visual example of a first then chart. *First,* complete work (an 8-year-old girl is sitting at a desk with her computer in front of her), and *then,* play with the preferred toy (a princess horse castle toy with three princess figurines on horses).

Weekly Goal Setting

Picking an IEP objective or two each week to focus on with your students and communicating that goal to parents and caregivers during the weekly meeting are extremely important. Having too many goals, assignments, and expectations has led to failure and reduced student motivation. Ensure the learning goal is aligned with the annual IEP goals, and, most importantly, the learning goal is reinforced throughout the week by both parents and educators. By verbalizing and displaying this learning goal, educators will help the students recognize the why behind the lesson, understand the expectations, work toward a specific accomplishment, and take ownership of achieving the goal. Keep the goal and expectation clear and concise.

IEP Walk-Through – Focus on PLEP A

Review or walk through the IEP with the parents and caregivers and commit to spending a reasonable amount of time explaining the Present Level of Educational Performance (PLEP A) section. PLEP A outlines the curriculum areas such as English Language Arts, History and Social Sciences, Science and Technology, Math, and Other Curriculum areas affected by the student's disability. There is also a section embedded in the PLEP A that explains and describes how the disability affects progress. Explaining the curriculum areas

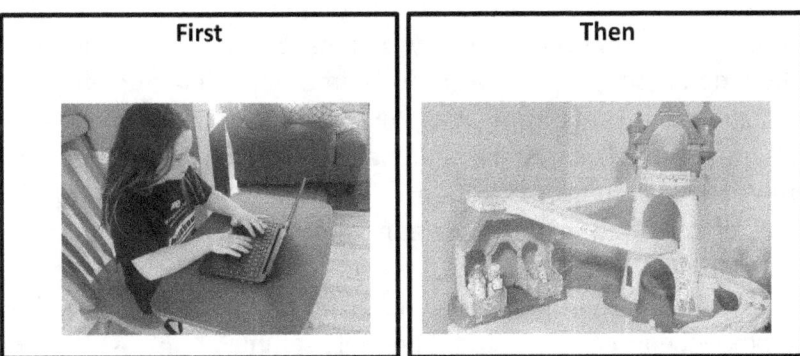

FIGURE 10.2 Example of a First Then Chart

affected by the disability and explaining how the specific disability affects progress are a critical section to share with parents. Doing so will help them understand common learning roadblocks at home and the subjects that their child may struggle in.

Another valuable part of PLEP A to educate parents on is the accommodations section. For anyone who is not a formally trained educator, the accommodation list might seem like a bulleted list of random actions and words, with some educational jargon thrown in for good measure. Whereas educators can look at those bullets and know precisely what to do to help the child be successful in school, most parents and caregivers will need guidance. Spend time with parents reviewing all the suggested accommodations and provide recommendations to help parents implement and replicate at home in the remote learning environment. Break down the accommodation for the parents by setting, presentation, timing/scheduling, and response. Explain each section by defining and providing appropriate examples using specific examples in terms parents and caregivers will understand and offer remote-friendly suggestions for each student's accommodations. (See Chapter 6 for common accommodations and the remote equivalent.)

The next section is an expansion of the PLEP A with some do it yourself (DIY) accommodations.

Sensory Tools

Sensory tools, which are objects, fidgets, putty, and other tools to stimulate the senses or focus on a single sensory input, are another popular way to provide sensory options. Studies have found that allowing sensory input during worktime improved students' participation and on-task behaviors (Noddings, 2017). Students with diagnoses, such as ADHD, anxiety, and autism, have shown improvements in concentration if they could fidget or use a tool that redirects the fidget. Integrating these tools in the classroom appropriately and explaining the expectations of their use to students can create a great learning environment for students. The same concepts can be used in a remote setting.

If resources are available, educators can create a personal sensory toolkit for each student with a few small tools delivered to the home or picked up at the school. If tools and resources to share are unavailable, educators can send home a letter to make DIY tools.

During school, many teachers have a specific area of their classroom dedicated to sensory tools. Educators often call these areas different names such as "Sensory Corners" or "Calm-Down Corners". Educators can include sensory tools for access when students need them or for breaks. With guidance from the educator, parents can replicate this idea at home and perhaps have an at-home sensory shelf or a sensory drawer to allow children access to during the day. Some items to include that can be found at home to fit in a sensory box or shelf could be:

Simple Hand and Feet Fidget Tools:

- Various textured cloth material.
- Squeeze balls and squishy toys of varying textures and firmness level.
- Bins of Putty, Play-Doh, Slime.
- Tupperware container of rice or kinetic sand.
- Tupperware container of nuts and bolts.
- Velcro strips to stick under the desk to feel during independent activities.
- Stretch/resistance bands to use at the bottom of chairs for fidgety feet.
- Tupperware container of beads.

Relaxation Tools:

- Headphones (noise-canceling, silent, or with soothing music).
- Lap weights/weighted blanket/weighted stuffed animals.
- Colored glasses/blue light glasses (help with visual input or block flickering of fluorescent lights).
- Bubbles to blow to regulate breathing and relaxation.
- Massage balls or a foam roller.

Many occupational therapists and special education teachers have noted the benefits of working with parents to create sensory boxes for remote instruction. Figure 10.3 is a sample sensory box, labeled

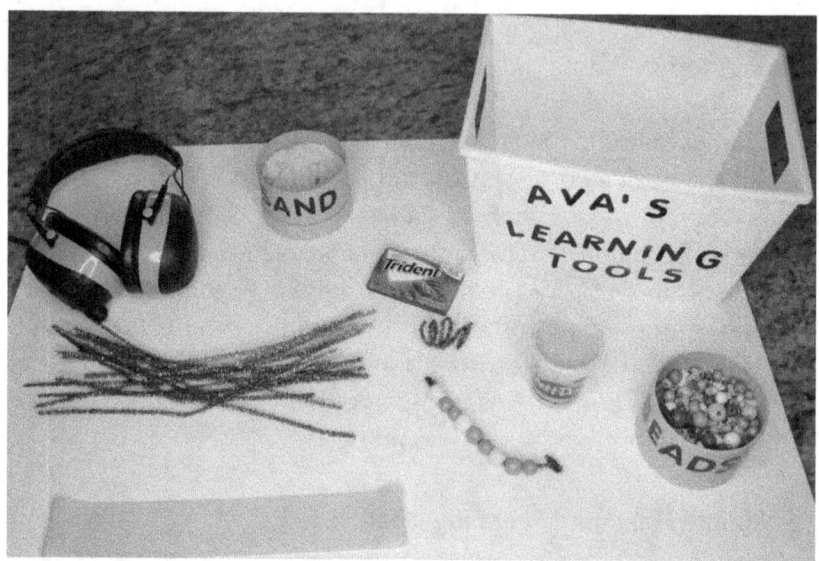

FIGURE 10.3 A Sample Sensory Box

as "Ava's Learning Tools". It is a white box with kinetic sand, pipe cleaners, noise-canceling headphones, beads, Play-Doh, a resistance band, and gum displayed on a white piece of cardboard.

Timers and Frequent Breaks

Timers and frequent breaks are useful strategies to educate parents and caregivers to improve the remote learning experience for everyone involved.

Timers keep children on task for a given amount of time. They can learn to independently start and reset the timers while progressing through their daily schedule. Once they move through and complete a certain timed amount of work, they earn a break. The break should be a preferred activity of the child's choice or an enjoyable brain break. Timers can also dictate when the break is over and it is time to get back to work. By utilizing timers at home during the day, ownership moves from the parent to the child. The parent is not just arbitrarily mandating that the child needs to get back to work. The timer does. The timer dictates when it is time to stop the break and get to work, leading to fewer child and parent arguments, frustrations, and defiant behaviors.

Breaks improve the cognitive ability and focus of students. Frequent physical movement breaks also allow students to regulate their behavior and emotions and provide the students with an opportunity to stimulate their sensory needs. When children have to sit and remain in one place, it is likely to result in fatigue and disruptive behavior (Levine, 2015; Brekke-Sisk, 2006). Incorporating movement breaks throughout the day can benefit from controlling sensory integration and improving readiness to learn. Incorporating movement breaks routinely rather than using them on a need-basis prevents behavior incidents before they start. Frequent breaks throughout the day are necessary, especially if children are sitting in front of a computer all day.

Make a list of suggested movement breaks that can be done at home and share that list with parents and caregivers. Some suggestions could be:

GoNoodle Videos, Koo Koo Kanga Roo, KIDZ BOP: YouTube has many kid-friendly movement videos ranging from quick videos that last only a minute or two to longer videos around 20 minutes. GoNoodle, Koo Koo Kango Roo, and KIDZ BOP offer movement breaks include songs with movement, dance videos, and exercise routines.

Outdoor Activity: Make a list of outdoor movement break ideas for students to refer to when a break is earned. Such activities could include jump rope, hopscotch, dancing, running, riding a bike, or spending a few minutes shooting basketballs, kicking soccer balls, or stickhandling a hockey puck.

Create a list for Outdoor Scavenger Hunts: Present parents with pre-made outdoor scavenger hunt activities that you, the educator, can participate in. For example, one day during a movement break, have students try to find a rock that looks like a heart or maybe a stick with three distinctive colors. During a synchronous meeting, the educator can ask the student if anyone did an outdoor scavenger hunt and share what they found. Knowing the outdoor environment, parents and caregivers could also create an outdoor scavenger hunt to use during breaks.

At-Home Sensory/Motor Paths: Many schools have sensory/motor paths that parents can replicate at home. Figure 10.4 is

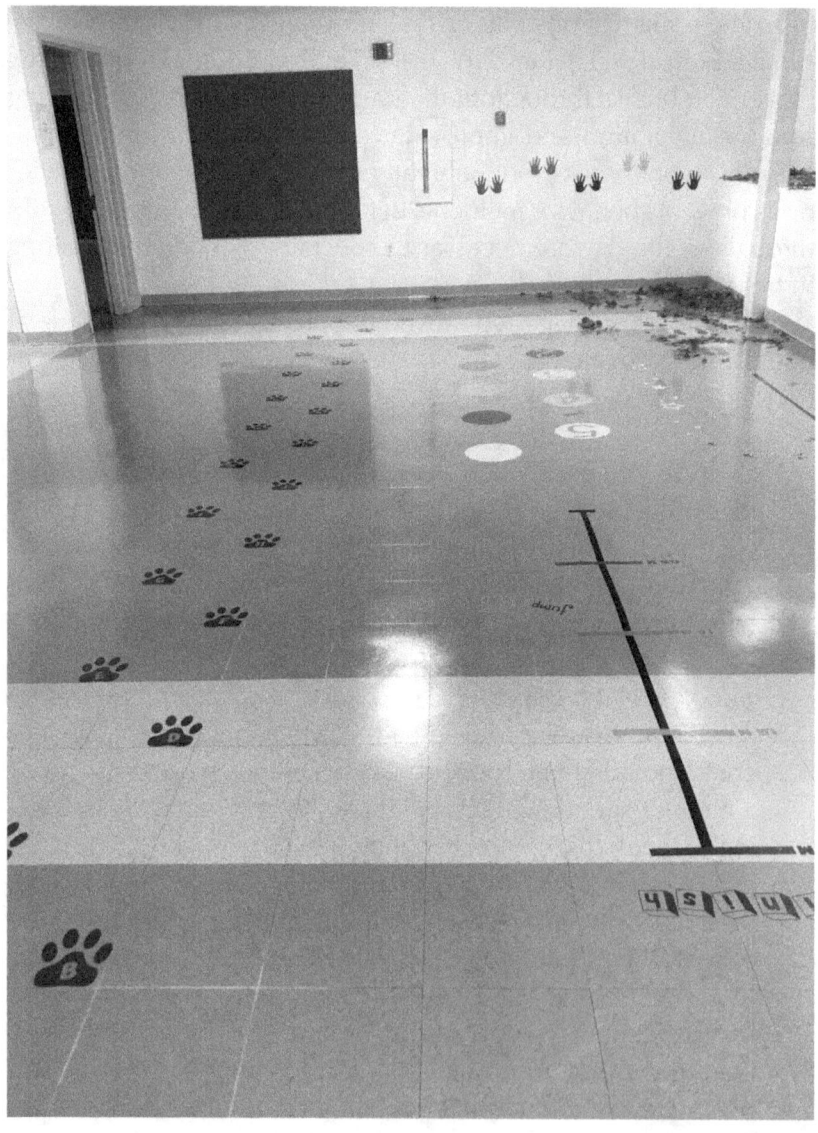

FIGURE 10.4 An At-School Motor Path

a picture of an at-school motor path. It is a school floor with A through Z paws, numbered circles 1 through 5, five other circles not numbered, and four lines with the word "jump". Five pairs of handprints are displayed on the far wall.

Parents can recreate motor paths by using painter's tape, duct tape, and construction paper. Figure 10.5 shows a simple at-home path created in a hallway of a house. The floor has a start sign with three small lines, two large lines, staggered circles, and a zigzag. Two pairs of handprints, labeled wall jump, and wall press are visible on the sidewall.

Work together with parents to discuss ideas to create a sensory/motor path using chalk outside or tape and construction paper. Using visuals, parents can add to the path and have children hop on one foot, do wall push-ups, skips, wall jumps, and frog jumps. The ideas are endless. Use the sensory path during the day as a sensory outlet or as a movement break. These act as an excellent brain break with high-intensity activities that enable students to return to work, improving focus for more extended periods.

Understanding Assistive Technology
Educating parents on the importance of assistive technology for remote instruction has been a useful share for parents. Educators do not have to spend too much time on this task because reputable teaching options are available for a parent to reference. For example, the Center on Technology and Disability offers an Introduction to Assistive Technology video that outlines essential topics, concepts, and ideas for using assistive technology with students with disabilities. The video is a great resource that can be viewed and shared at no cost.

Here is the link: www.ctdinstitute.org/library/2017-10-05/intro-assistive-technology-video

FIGURE 10.5 A Simple At-Home Path

Success Story

Andrew, a father from New Hampshire, presets his home Alexa device to alarm for his son's brain and motor breaks. He sets the Alexa device so the day is consistent, and every day (five times a day) at the exact same time, Alexa alarms, and his son knows he has a ten-minute break. He works with his son's special education teacher to be consistent and aware of the plan. This works for the family because Andrew works from home and would forget to remind his son of breaks. With breaks preset through Alexa, his son has been more independent and does not rely on him to dictate breaks.

Quick Tips From Educators

Jackie, an occupational therapist from Colorado, recommends sharing DIY sensory tool ideas with parents. Parents have told Jackie that they appreciate her sensory tool DIY suggestions. One of the easiest, do it yourself fidget tools are "pipe cleaner fingers". Use a pipe cleaner to wrap around a finger or two. The child can feel the texture while independently working and increase focus on the task at hand. This is a budget-friendly alternative to some of the expensive fidget tools out there. Parents have told Jackie that pipe cleaner fingers have been working well.

Natalie, a grades 3–4 special education teacher from New York, recommends that parents start each day and end each day with structure. Before everyone signs in for work and school, it has been beneficial to sit down with their children to go over the daily schedule and answer any questions their children may have. She also recommends reconvening at the end of the remote school day to note successes and challenges and document them. Documenting success and challenges is essential and helpful for the teacher and the parent. Natalie meets weekly with parents and relies on those successes and challenges when planning the next weeks' lesson and activities focusing on the child's success.

 Highlighted Resources

External Parent Training and Support Groups:

Here are some supports retrieved from the Massachusetts Department of Secondary and Elementary Education (2020) that can be shared with families:

- The Center for Excellence in Developmental Disabilities (CEDD) provides educational resources on developmental disabilities to the community. CEDD has sponsored educational videos and online training modules, such as ADEPT (Autism Distance Education Parent Training) Interactive Learning. ADEPT has a ten-lesson interactive, self-paced, online learning module for parents. The training includes tools to more effectively teach their child with autism and disabilities functional skills using applied behavior analysis (ABA) techniques. It can be found here: https://health.ucdavis.edu/mindinstitute/centers/cedd/adept.html
- A support group offered through the Home for Little Wanderers offers parent support and group discussion for families caring for children with behavioral and mental health needs. www.thehome.org/site/PageNavigator/ParentSupportProgram.html
- The American Academy of Pediatrics has put out an advisory to help parents facing stress during remote learning. The advisory stressed that parents and caregivers must practice self-care and reach out to others for support. https://services.aap.org/en/news-room/news-releases/aap/2020/the-american-academy-of-pediatrics-advises-parents-experiencing-stress-over-covid-19/
- Additionally, the Child Mind Institute offers phone consultations, video talks, and other resources for families

dealing with the stress related to COVID-19 and related remote instruction. https://childmind.org/coping-during-covid-19-resources-for-parents/

 Remember

✓ Educators and parents should work together and figure out solutions to help the child succeed.
✓ Remember, empathy – Parents fear their children are falling behind academically and missing developmental milestones while losing the life skills necessary for independent living.
✓ Help parents create a learning space, agendas, and routines.
✓ Walk through and highlight important areas of the IEPs and together establish a home school weekly goal.
✓ Sensory input during worktime improved the participation and on-task behaviors of students. Share DIY sensory tools and brain break ideas with parents.

References

Brekke-Sisk, N. (2006). Standing-room only in the classroom of the future. *Mayo Clinic Magazine.* Retrieved from https://mcforms.mayo.edu/mc4400-mc4499/mc4409-0906.pdf

Jacobson, L. (2020, July 29). *Parents (and lawyers) say distance learning failed too many special education students. As fall approaches, families wonder if their children will lose another school year.* Retrieved from www.the74million.org/article/parents-and-lawyers-say-distance-learning-failed-too-many-special-education-students-as-fall-approaches-families-wonder-if-their-children-will-lose-another-school-year/

Kamentz, A. (2020, July 23). *Families of children with special needs are suing in several states: Here's why.* National Public Radio. Retrieved from www.npr.org/2020/07/23/893450709/families-of-children-with-special-needs-aresuing-in-several-states-heres-why

Levine, J. A. (2015). Sick of sitting. *Diabetologia, 58*(8), 1751–1758. https://doi.org/10.1007/s00125-015-3624-6

Noddings, A. (2017). Classroom solutions for sensory-sensitive students. *Montessori Life*, *29*(2), 44–49.

Rhode Island Parent Information Network. (2020). *Distance learning and special education survey*. Retrieved from https://ripin.org/distance-learning-special-education-parent-survey/

Conclusion: Bringing It All Together

Educators' patience, resilience, strength, adaptability, and passion for educating have all been put to the test. Every single one of them not only stepped up to the plate, ready to take on the unknown, but they have all gone above and beyond for our children. For that, I am immensely grateful.

– Vanessa France, Jack's Mom

The progression of educating children with disabilities and learning challenges in a remote environment is an area for continuous improvement and further exploration. Ongoing research and continued development will be necessary to successfully implement remote learning for students with Individualized Education Programs (IEPs), especially as the educational landscape continues to change and offers more opportunities for remote learning. Successfully teaching children who require special education services relies heavily on trial and error, reflection, and purposeful relationship development. The strategies provided here are based on ideas and examples shared by educators who found them helpful and effective, and they should be customized to meet each student's specific educational and emotional needs and to align with the educators' preferred style and approach.

In the calibration of survey results, interviews, and document gathering, the overarching suggestions for a successful foundation for remote instruction for students with IEPs identified four significant recommendations for all remote special education programs.

- ♦ Building relationships within the special education community is critical for the success, participation, accountability, and ownership of learning and growth for students with IEPs.
- ♦ Creating opportunities for parent engagement and partnership is imperative for the consistency and reinforcement of all goals such as academic, behavioral, occupational

therapy (OT), physical therapy (PT), speech and language, and other IEP service delivery goals.
- Open communication and tracking communication among the entire IEP team, including parents and paraprofessionals, are essential to keeping track of goal progression, expectations, and all other information regarding accessibility and engagement.
- Developing a special education program around consistent routines and structures is essential in the remote environment.

In an analysis of the successful strategies provided by over 250 educators, those four areas were dominant and proved imperative when creating an effective remote classroom for students with IEPs.

Building Relationships

Building relationships within the special education community is crucial for the success, participation, accountability, and ownership of learning and growth for students with IEPs. Relationship building cannot be done in isolation and needs to be prioritized among all the stakeholders involved in the education of a child requiring special education services. Teachers should begin the year by concentrating on relationship building with students to emphasize mutual respect, empathy, and understanding. Building relationships also applies to relationships among educators and parents, service providers, and paraprofessionals. Working together as a collaborative unit with a student-centered mindset will improve remote learning for children with Individualized Education Programs.

Parent Engagement

It is without question that parent involvement is critical to improving remote learning for students with IEPs. Educators mentioned its importance throughout each section of the guidebook. The key is to create opportunities that promote students' independence to attend classes daily while creating opportunities for parent engagement around parent schedules, availability, and ease of participation. The added responsibilities are extremely challenging for parents, and acknowledging those challenges in creative ways is appreciated. Creating opportunities for parent engagement and home partnership is imperative for the consistency and reinforcement of academic, behavioral, occupational therapy, physical therapy, speech and language services, and other IEP service delivery goals.

Communication

Open communication and tracking communication among the entire IEP team, parents, and paraprofessionals are essential to record goal progression, expectations, and all other information regarding the student's accessibility and engagement. Typically, a student with an IEP has a team of individuals working together with the child's success as a core priority that keeps the group in contact. In the remote environment, the interactions and opportunities to communicate are less frequent. In addition to scheduled days and times to meet, having communication documents to track interactions and conversations is helpful. Formalizing meetings with agendas, roles, and norms ensures that the allotted time for communication remains student-focused and targeted.

Consistent Routines

Developing a special education program around consistent routines and structures is just as crucial in the remote environment as it is in person. Routine and consistency create a structure necessary to establish a caring, safe, nurturing environment with a positive culture. An unstructured day with a schedule and routine changes will create chaos. Students benefit from a posted schedule with a predictable routine, color-coded materials, and all links and expectations visible and easy to access in the remote classroom. Not only will they create an order for the school day, but consistent routines and structure will also promote independence.

Final Thought

The strategies provided by the educators throughout the chapters made it clear that no one can work in isolation. With a focus on student growth and achievement, an organized, collaborative, and structured approach to working with students is necessary. With the shared strategies, educators can create a foundation of knowledge, further develop their practice, and share their successes to help colleagues. The global pandemic of 2020 proved that we are experiencing historical changes in education, confirming that many of our practices before 2020 are outdated. Within the devastation of school closures, a number of innovative approaches have been developed to take with us into the future of education, including different modalities and learning techniques for all learners and abilities. Eventually, the 2020 pandemic will be a distant memory, and life will return to normal, but education as we know it is forever altered.

Thank You

As Mr. Rogers famously stated,

> most of my childhood heroes wore capes, flew through the air, or picked up buildings with one arm.... But as I grew, my heroes changed, so that now I can honestly say that anyone who does anything to help a child is a hero to me.

In 2020 amidst a global pandemic, it become clearly evident that educators are selfless heroes. A collection of heroes contributed to this guidebook and took time out of their busy schedules to share successful strategies to help the larger community. I will forever be thankful for the energy and efforts of the contributing educators and parents. Your insight and experiences are eye-opening, and your contributions to the future of education will help our children who need them most. Thank you!

For Product Safety Concerns and Information please contact our EU
representative GPSR@taylorandfrancis.com
Taylor & Francis Verlag GmbH, Kaufingerstraße 24, 80331 München, Germany